OutStaNDing
mini albums

▶ **50** *ideas* for
creating mini scrapbooks

Jessica Acs

MEMORY
MAKERS
BOOKS

Cincinnati, Ohio
www.mycraftivity.com

About the Author

First, inspired by a scrapbook her sister made more than 10 years ago, Jessica has been hooked on scrapbooking ever since. She especially enjoys creating mini albums and teaches classes on them at scrapbook stores as well as at conventions. One of the founders and president of the International Scrapbooking Association (www.WeScrap.com), Jess was born and raised in beautiful Victoria, British Columbia, Canada. She is currently living happily in Vancouver with her fiancé, Brent, and favorite scrapbooking subjects, their cute terriers, Angus and Zoey. They also have other small pets that are featured in many of her mini books. When she's not scrapbooking, Jess enjoys spending time with family and friends, traveling, shopping and exploring new places around British Columbia with Brent and their dogs.

Outstanding Mini Albums. Copyright© 2009 by Jessica Acs. Manufactured in the USA. All rights reserved. It is permissible for the purchaser to make the projects contained herein and sell them at fairs, bazaars and craft shows. No other part of this book may be reproduced in any form or by any electronic or mechanical means including information storage and retrieval systems without permission in writing from the publisher, except by a reviewer, who may quote a brief passage in review. Published by Memory Makers Books, an imprint of F+W Media, Inc., 4700 East Galbraith Road, Cincinnati, Ohio 45236. (800) 289-0963. First edition.

13 12 11 10   6 5 4 3

Distributed in Canada by Fraser Direct
100 Armstrong Avenue
Georgetown, ON, Canada L7G 5S4
Tel: (905) 877-4411

Distributed in the U.K. and Europe by David & Charles
Brunel House, Newton Abbot, Devon, TQ12 4PU, England
Tel: (+44) 1626 323200, Fax: (+44) 1626 323319
E-mail: postmaster@davidandcharles.co.uk

Distributed in Australia by Capricorn Link
P.O. Box 704, S. Windsor, NSW 2756 Australia
Tel: (02) 4577-3555

Library of Congress Cataloging-in-Publication Data

Acs, Jessica.
  Outstanding mini albums : 50 ideas for creating mini scrapbooks / by Jessica Acs. -- 1st ed.
    p. cm.
  Includes bibliographical references and index.
  ISBN 978-1-59963-032-8 (pbk. : alk. paper)
  1. Photograph albums. 2. Photographs--Conservation and restoration. 3. Scrapbooking.
  4. Miniature craft. I. Title.
  TR501.A28 2009
  745.593--dc22

                    2008034797

fw media
www.fwmedia.com

Metric Conversion Chart

to convert	to	multiply by
Inches	Centimeters	2.54
Centimeters	Inches	0.4
Feet	Centimeters	30.5
Centimeters	Feet	0.03
Yards	Meters	0.9
Meters	Yards	1.1
Sq. Inches	Sq. Centimeters	6.45
Sq. Centimeters	Sq. Inches	0.16
Sq. Feet	Sq. Meters	0.09
Sq. Meters	Sq. Feet	10.8
Sq. Yards	Sq. Meters	0.8
Sq. Meters	Sq. Yards	1.2
Pounds	Kilograms	0.45
Kilograms	Pounds	2.2
Ounces	Grams	28.3
Grams	Ounces	0.035

Editor: Kristin Boys
Designer: Kelly O'Dell
Art Coordinator: Eileen Aber
Production Coordinator: Greg Nock
Photographers: Ric Deliantoni, Adam Hand, Christine Polomsky
Stylist: Nora Martini

Dedication & Acknowledgments

Dedication For my mother, Carolyn. Thank you for introducing me to the crafting world when I was very young, for helping and encouraging me throughout the development of this book, and for endlessly loving me. You continue to inspire me with your projects, and without your help and support, this book would not have been possible.

Acknowledgments Thank you to both my parents for always supporting me in whatever endeavors I choose to take part in, and for knowing that there is no stopping me when I have my heart set on something! You both mean the world to me. I love you and will forever be grateful for everything you have done for me.

Thank you to all my family and friends for putting up with me during this adventure and for letting me use photos of you in this book.

Thank you to my loving fiancé, Brent, for your support, encouragement, love and fabulous photos. Thanks for letting me pursue my dream.

Thank you to the contributing designers: Cami Bauman, Kathie Davis, Andrea Deer, Carolyn Lontin, Brenda Neuberger, Julie Overby, Mou Saha and Michelle Van Etten. You are all so inspiring, and I feel honored to have your work featured in this book.

Thank you to the wonderful team at F+W who all had a part in making this book come to life. I am completely amazed by the amount of talent each of you have, and I thoroughly enjoyed meeting all of you when I was in Cincinnati.

Finally, a special thank you to my fabulous editor, Kristin Boys, for guiding me through this exciting process (and for introducing me to Graeter's ice cream!). And thank you to my amazing photographer, Christine Polomsky, for taking such awesome photos of my mini books in the making (and reminding me to keep rolling my sleeves up!), and to Christine Doyle for believing in me.

3 chapter

4 chapter

reduce,
REUSE, RECYCLE

think outside
THE BOX

62 *Making Mini Albums out of Everyday Items*

96 *Crafting Unique Mini Album Gifts*

an addiction
IS BORN

While visiting San Francisco, I ate at a restaurant with friends one night. Our server brought coasters to the table with each drink and by the time we left, the table had accumulated quite a number of coasters. I grabbed them all while we were leaving, and when everyone looked at me with odd expressions, I explained that (of course!) I might be able to do something scrapbooking-related with them.

To prove that I could do what I said I would, after I returned home to Canada, I went to work creating my first mini album—out of the leftover coasters. Two new addictions were born that day: one to making mini albums and one to using a Crop-A-Dile punch. That first little mini album stirred something within me. Mini albums became my sole scrapping projects, and I started teaching classes at my local scrapbook store.

Mini albums are still pretty much all I want to make. There is nothing better then being able to sit down and finish an entire album in one sitting. With an endless number of possible themes, mini albums are so much fun and practical for any set of photos. I find them easier to display than larger albums, and they are fantastic to make as gifts for people, too. In this book, I've included all my favorite types of mini books with photo instructions for creating them. I hope you enjoy making them as much as I do, and maybe your own addiction will be born!

Before You Begin

Tools & Materials

Outside, clockwise from upper left: Bind-it-All machine, Crop-A-Dile, trimmer with scoring and cutting blades, paper piercer, bone folder, sponge brush, bulldog clips, chalk ink, brayer. Middle, left to right: binder rings, set of sanding tools, wet and dry adhesive.

You can make many of the mini albums in this book with basics like scissors, glue and a hole punch. But the following tools will make the process a snap, plus help you finish your pages with perfection!

Trimmer with scoring blade: A must for easily cutting and scoring straight lines.

Bone folder: A handy tool to set creases for perfect, clean folds.

Wet and dry adhesives: A glue like Zip Dry works well for projects because it holds firmly. Thin double-sided tape is useful for creating pockets on pages, envelopes and virtually anything else.

Brayer: This really helps to eliminate air bubbles when you are attaching paper to mini album pages.

Sponge brush: Inexpensive and easy to wash and reuse, it makes applying acrylic paint and decoupage medium a snap.

Bulldog clips: Use these to hold papers together while adhesive is drying. Plus, they make great embellishments!

Paper piercer: I often use this versatile little tool to unclog adhesive bottle tips and punch holes before hand stitching or inserting brads.

Crop-A-Dile: A must-have for many of the albums in this book. It is hands down the best hole punch I have ever used! It punches through chipboard like butter, and it will also punch through CDs, thin metal and more!

Small chalk ink pad: This makes inking edges easy and comes in a variety of colors.

Sanding tools: Sanding sponges smooth rough edges and prep materials for adhesive. Thin sanding tools are great for getting into tiny grooves.

Binder rings: Rings come in lots of sizes and colors and are great for binding mini albums made from scratch. You can also hang charms and embellishments from rings.

Bind-it-All: This fabulous little machine made by Zutter will turn any little book you create into a spiral-bound masterpiece!

How to Score with a Trimmer

Many of the projects in this book will require you to score strips of paper. I find using the Fiskars 12" (30cm) trimmer with scoring blade is the easiest way to score. Follow the directions below to understand how to read the scoring measurements in the book's step-by-step instructions. This example shows you how to score a 4" × 12" (10cm × 30cm) strip of paper from the left edge at 5½" and 9¾" (14cm × 25cm).

5½" mark

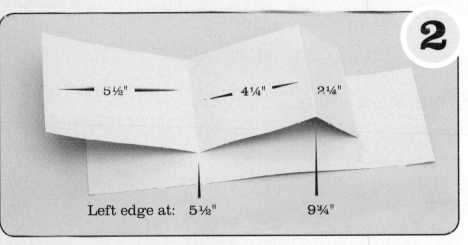

5½"   4¼"   2¼"

Left edge at: 5½"   9¾"

1. Place and score the strip
Open the trimmer's arm. Then set the strip of paper in the trimmer horizontally. Move the left edge of the strip to the 5½" (14cm) mark at the top of the trimmer. Score the paper. Then move the strip so that the left edge of the strip is at 9¾" (25cm). Score the paper.

2. Check that scoring is correct
You should end up with three sections separated by a score line: a 5½" (14cm) section, a 4¼" (11cm) section and a 2¼" (6cm) section.

About the Materials List
Sheets of chipboard, cardstock and patterned paper, unless otherwise specified, are 12" × 12" (30cm × 30cm).

When projects call for chipboard, any kind you have on hand will do. Crafty Board (by WorldWin) works well, as does chipboard left over from paper packaging.

You can use whatever adhesive you like for each project, unless it calls for a specific type. When a project requires liquid glue, choose one like Zip Dry (by Beacon Adhesives) that comes with a precision tip.

1

chapter

BUGS

make
YOUR MARK

Decorating Pre-Made Mini Albums

With the variety of mini album shapes, materials and sizes available, it's no secret that mini albums are a hot topic. What's better than being able to get an entire scrapbook album done in a day? But even with store-bought, pre-bound albums, the opportunities for making your mark are only limited by your imagination. And the choice of mini album themes is just as endless—you can scrap just about any topic you can think of, like my wise words on page 14 and Mou Saha's obsession with chocolate on page 25. So go pick up your pre-made album of choice and create a fabulous mini book in a snap! All you need are some photos, your favorite supplies and a little creativity.

Binder Albums

Andrea created this fun sports-themed ABC book for her young son. She was hoping it would be a creative way for him to learn his ABCs (or "CBCs" as he calls them), and since he loves sports, this theme was the perfect fit. Andrea gave each letter its own page featuring a sports-related word and bright colors.

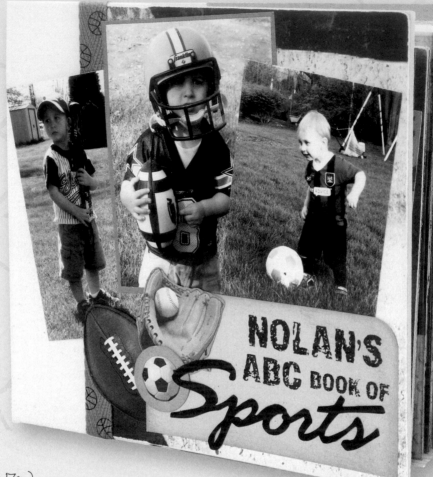

Actual size: 7¾" × 6½" (18cm × 17cm)

Supplies: Cardstock; patterned paper, rub-ons (Scrappin' Sports); stickers (Paper Studio, Scrappin' Sports); chipboard accents (Fancy Pants); twill (Creative Impressions); die-cut shapes (Provo Craft, Sizzix); ink (Clearsnap)

Artwork by Andrea Deer

I used classic wedding colors—black and white—for the color scheme of this mini binder album to allow the pictures to stand out. The featured bride and groom are friends who were married in Hawaii. The bride's wedding gown was a beautiful green instead of the traditional white, so using black-and-white pages as the backdrop makes the striking colors in the photos pop.

Actual size: 7" × 6½" (18cm × 17cm)

Supplies: Album (BoBunny); cardstock; patterned paper (Doodlebug, KI Memories, Pebbles, Stemma); embellishments (American Crafts, Making Memories, Stemma); rub-ons, stickers (American Crafts, BoBunny, Lasting Impressions, Making Memories); ribbon, twine (Adornit, Creative Imaginations, Creative Impressions); inks (Close to My Heart, Clearsnap, Tsukineko); pens (American Crafts)

Album Technique

Ribbon Closure

Who doesn't need a little advice from time to time? When I came across this little mini chipboard album by Maya Road, I immediately realized it would make a great addition to my mini book collection. Because of its small pages and simple design, I opted to make a book of wise words for my nieces, pairing quotes with photos I had on hand. Adding a ribbon closure to the album ties everything together perfectly. And you can use this technique to put a pretty finishing touch on any type of album.

Actual size: 5" × 4" (13cm × 10cm)

Supplies: Album (Maya Road); patterned paper (BasicGrey); arrow accent (Scenic Route); ribbon (May Arts); inks (Clearsnap, Tsukineko); pens (American Crafts, Sakura, Uni-ball); adhesive (Beacon)

Materials

chipboard album	brayer
ribbon (at least 12" [30cm])	craft knife (optional)
scissors	sanding sponge
adhesive	hole punch (⅛" [3mm]) or Crop-A-Dile
patterned paper (1 sheet)	

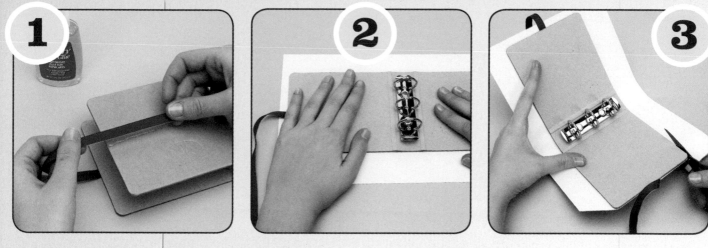

1. Attach ribbon to covers

Remove the inside pages of the album and set them aside. Cut the piece of ribbon in half. Adhere about 1" of ribbon to the front cover; repeat this step on the back cover. (Ribbon pieces will be used to tie the book together.)

2. Adhere paper to covers

Open the binder and apply adhesive to the outside. Then place it flat on the back of the patterned paper. Use the brayer to smooth the paper to prevent air bubbles.

3. Trim and sand edges

Once the adhesive dries, trim excess paper off the edges of the album using scissors or a craft knife. Use a sanding sponge to smooth all the edges of the album.

Hand-Drawn Letters

Draw your own letters to lend a childlike charm to kid-friendly albums.

Spiral-Bound Albums

As I flipped through this adorable ABC book that Mou created for her two-year-old son, I kept asking myself, "How did she do that?" I love the way she incorporated colored pencils, stamps and embellishments on her pages. Mou made this little book to record memorable details about her son at age two so she doesn't forget those little things once he moves on to the next stage.

Actual size: 4¼" × 4" (11cm × 10cm)

Supplies: Buttons, chipboard letters, mini book, patterned paper (Rusty Pickle); stamps (Inque Boutique); ink (Ranger); color pencils (ChartPak)

Artwork by Mou Saha

a day in the life of Jack

Brenda's idea to document a day in her son's life made for a fabulous mini album! She started by choosing a day and taking photos of Jack doing all the things he usually does. She put them all together into a mini album for a complete "day in the life" snapshot! Try Brenda's idea to add a unique twist to your own mini album: Tie a large chipboard letter to the album spine with bits of ribbon scraps.

Actual size: 5" × 6¾" (13cm × 17cm)

Supplies: Album, buttons, chipboard accents, patterned paper, stickers, trim (Rusty Pickle); die-cut letters (Provo Craft); Misc: acrylic paint, pen

Artwork by Brenda Neuberger

Boy! ···Oh Boy! ···Oh Boy! ···Oh Boy! ···Oh Boy!

INGREDIENTS: SNIPS, SNAILS AND PUPPY DOG TAILS

nap

3:30 pm

100 % GENUINE BOY

4:00 pm

playing

Scallop-Edge 2-Ring Albums

Artwork by Carolyn Lontin

This album really caught my eye when I first saw it. I don't think I've ever seen a mini album on bugs before—and this one was so irresistibly cute! Carolyn's son loves bugs, so she created this album to celebrate his love of nature. After collecting photos for about a year, she was able to finish off the book. I especially love the cute little bug die-cuts she's added—adorable fun!

Actual size: 4" × 5" (10cm × 13cm)

Supplies: Chipboard swirls, mini album (Maya Road); cardstock; patterned paper (KI Memories); flowers (Bazzill); chipboard letters (Heidi Swapp); chipboard accents (Magistical Memories); journal cards (Luxe); ribbon (Strano); die-cuts (Sizzix)

Artwork by Mou Saha

I admire Mou's ability to make a simple book so beautiful and detailed. She created this album to honor an important time in her young daughter's life: becoming a reader. With her fabulous handwriting on painted chipboard pages, Mou documented the course of events that led them to the milestone achievement.

Actual size: 6" × 6" (15cm × 15cm)

Supplies: Chipboard album, letter stickers, patterned paper (Rusty Pickle); chipboard letters (Heidi Swapp); chipboard tag (KI Memories); chipboard stars (Making Memories); acrylic paint (Delta), ink (Ranger); pen (American Crafts)

I wanted to keep the tradition alive — My dad used to read out loud his novels so we (mom and I) could enjoy too — mom, while she tackled chores and me as I painted. I cannot imagine life without books and knowing that Ashis is not an avid reader, I realized that it was going to be mainly my responsibility to imbue in my kids a love of reading.

By the time, you were six months old, you had a library card. Ashis thought I was crazy. My mom thought it was a step in the right direction ... and kinda cute. Well, thanks to the public library system of our county, there was a "Baby's First Book" gift in the essential baby care package from the hospital along with a library card application form.

3-Ring Album

Michelle took a plain wooden album and made it sparkle with loads of glitter and bling. Michelle's album provides a glimpse into the life of a mother with a child on the autistic spectrum. Every day with her son, James, is a new adventure for Michelle, and he has taught her to be grateful for their many blessings. She shares lessons learned from James in this album that really shines.

Actual size: 6½" × 6½" (17cm × 17cm)

Supplies: Album, chipboard letters, flowers, rhinestones (Prima); cardstock; patterned paper (Autumn Leaves, Daisy D's, K&Co.. Prima); labels (Dymo); file folder, tabs (Sizzix); tags (Daisy D's); tag punch (EK Success); ribbon (Creative Impressions, Junkitz, Prima); ink (Clearsnap)

Artwork by Michelle Van Etten

20

I love the way Cami used newspaper as patterned paper, accenting it with pinks and browns to create a unique and fabulous look. To finish off the girly design, she added bling and lace to the pages. It's a fantastic album that begs to be touched over and over again!

Actual size: 5¼" × 6" (13cm × 15cm)

Supplies: Buttons, chipboard album and shapes, patterned paper, ribbon, stamps, stickers, tags (Rusty Pickle); cardstock; chipboard letters (Heidi Swapp, Rusty Pickle); rhinestones (Heidi Swapp); glitter glue (Ranger); rub-ons (Creative Imaginations); ink (Clearsnap); pen (Uni-ball)

Artwork by Cami Bauman

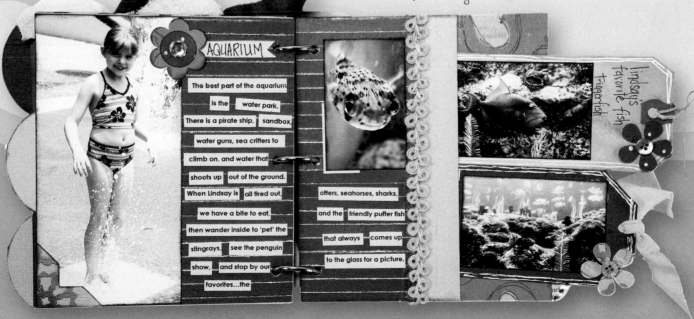

Mix-It-Up 3-Ring Album

Artwork by Kathie Davis

The theme of this mini album is a great idea for those who have kids and want to remember the funny things they say. Kathie's album documents some of her favorites—and they really are funny! I had a great time laughing my way through the pages. Kathie's album is bright and energetic, just like the children featured in it. Plus, Kathie used various shaped chipboard pieces for her pages, which really make the album unique.

Actual size: 6½" × 6" (17cm × 15cm)

Supplies: Album, buttons, chipboard accents (Rusty Pickle); patterned paper (Rusty Pickle, SEI); Misc: decorative punch, non-skid shelf liner

Bracket-Shaped Ring Album

I love Christmas. It gives me a valid reason to spoil my beloved pets. Before our annual visit with Santa last year, I decided to help them write a special letter to the Big Elf himself, expressing all their Christmas hopes and dreams. This cheerful little chipboard album is the result. I used a chipboard album by BasicGrey, seasonal paper, a variety of Christmas embellishments and, of course, comments and memories from Angus and Zoey.

Actual size: 5¾" × 5¾" (15cm × 15cm)

Supplies: Chipboard album (BasicGrey); patterned paper (Reminisce, Scenic Route); letter stickers, ribbon (American Crafts); sticker accents (KI Memories); chipboard and die-cut shapes (Scenic Route); transparent holiday shapes (Making Memories); ink (Clearsnap); pens (Sakura, Sanford); Misc: fabric strips

Acrylic 3-Ring Album

Clear albums are all the rage, and I have to admit I haven't had much of a chance to dabble in them. So as soon as I saw Julie's clear album by Pageframe, I knew I had to share it. Julie created this album so her kids could have some photos of her with them all having fun together. Thanks to Julie for this great tip: To adhere paper to clear pages, use paint! That way, both sides of the page will look great.

Artwork by Julie Overby

Actual size: 7½" × 6½" (19cm × 17cm)

Supplies: Album (Pageframe); cardstock; patterned paper (BasicGrey, Collage Press, Creative Imaginations); overlays (Hambly, My Mind's Eye); rub-ons (Daisy D's, Hambly, K&Co.); chipboard letters (American Crafts); rhinestones (Heidi Swapp, Me & My Big Ideas, Prima); die-cut shapes, paint (Making Memories); ribbon (Close to My Heart, Heidi Grace, Maya Road, Offray, Queen & Co.); stickers (EK Success, Heidi Grace, Making Memories, Scenic Route); stamps (Autumn Leaves, Fancy Pants); flowers (Doodlebug, Prima); buttons (Autumn Leaves); ink (Tsukineko)

Accordion-Fold Album in Pocket

It's a mini album all about chocolate! How could I not love it to little chocolate bits? Mou created this album about her chocolate obsession to document how she includes chocolate in every part of her day. I love Mou's creativity and the simple embellishments that finish off the album. Not only is this album delightful to look at, it makes my chocolate craving stronger by the second!

Artwork by Mou Saha

Actual size: 6" × 4¼" (15cm × 11cm)

Supplies: Album, patterned paper, photo turns, stickers, tabs, trims (Rusty Pickle); ink (Ranger)

Chalkboard Cover + Handmade Buttons

Actual size: 8½ × 5' (22cm × 13cm)

Supplies: Album (Junkitz); cardstock (WorldWin); patterned paper (A2Z, Adornit, Doodlebug, Pebbles, Sweetwater); ribbons (Creative Imaginations, Creative Impressions); stickers (Me & My Big Ideas); rub-ons (American Crafts, Doodlebug); brads (Imaginisce); label (Dymo); tabs (Colorbok); stapler (Close to My Heart); chalkboard paint (Tilano Fresco); ink (Close to My Heart, Clearsnap, Tsukineko); pen (Elmer's, Uni-ball); adhesive (Beacon)

When I bought this adorable Junkitz Rulerz album, I instantly thought of creating a school-themed book. My mum kept many mementos from my school days, which I scanned and resized so they could make it into the album along with school photos. The perfect finishing touches? Chalkboard paint by Tilano Fresco, which I used to paint the covers of this album to make them look like little blackboards. And handmade buttons made from Fimo—a type of polymer clay—in bright, primary colors to highlight the childhood theme.

Materials

Chalkboard
chalkboard paint
sponge brush
white paint pen

Buttons
polymer clay
paper piercer
paint or thread (optional)

Chalkboard Cover

1. Brush on paint
Paint the covers of your album with black chalkboard paint using the sponge brush. Let the paint dry, then apply a second coat.

2. Add lettering
After the second coat has dried, you are free to add the title of your book. Use the white paint pen to mimic the look of chalk—but without the smudging!

A Childlike Touch
For my childhood-themed album, I backed handmade polymer clay buttons with discs of felt.

Handmade Buttons

1. Shape clay
Shape the clay into small discs approximately the size of a quarter.

2. Poke holes and let clay dry
Poke four holes in the button using the paper piercer. Bake the buttons according to the manufacturer's instructions. Then add paint or thread, if desired.

2

chapter

[g|r|s]

ROAD TRIP

back to
SQUARE ONE

Creating Mini Albums from Scratch

Mini album mania isn't limited to books you can buy in the store. A little folding and cutting are all you really need to create your own mini albums from scratch. Sure, you have to start from the beginning, but making an entire album with your own hands is so rewarding! Just like store-bought mini albums, those you create from scratch can be crafted into loads of shapes, styles and themes, like Dasha's candy-colored birthday accordion book (on page 34) and my sisters album (on page 50) made with flower power. Plus, making your albums from square one gives you a reason to stock up on chipboard, hcavy-weight paper and colored cardstock—and who doesn't like a good excuse to go shopping?

House Album

As a child I loved hearing the story of the three little pigs and their flimsy homes. Having three little pigs (the guinea kind) of my own inspired me to make a mini album loosely based on the tale. I filled the house-shaped pages with photos of my piggies and their homes and added fairytale-style text. I love my little piggie house, but don't let my theme determine yours! You could make a "new home" album, a "my hometown" album or a "welcome" album for new neighbors. Whatever you do, this little book is perfect to house your creativity!

Materials
❈ House Template (page 124)
❈ chipboard (1 sheet)
❈ cardstock (1 sheet)
❈ patterned paper (2 sheets)
❈ pen or pencil
❈ scissors or craft knife
❈ paper trimmer (optional)
❈ adhesive
❈ sanding sponge
❈ hole punch or Crop-A-Dile
❈ binder rings

Actual size: 4½" × 7" (11cm × 18cm)

Supplies: Cardstock, crafty board (WorldWin); patterned paper (KI Memories); rub-ons, stickers (American Crafts, Arctic Frog, Doodlebug, Scenic Route); buttons (Creative Imaginations, Hero Arts, other); pen, ribbon (American Crafts); flower (Creative Imaginations); binder rings (Junkitz)

1. Trace and cut out template
Enlarge and trace the House Template (on page 124) twice onto chipboard. Then trace the template once onto cardstock. Cut out all three pieces.

2. Cut cardstock squares
Cut two pieces of cardstock to 4½" × 4½" (11cm × 11cm). The three pieces of cardstock (these two squares and the house shape) are your inside pages.

3. Add paper to covers
Adhere patterned paper to both sides of the two chipboard house shapes. (I used one pattern on the "roof" and one on the bottom.) Trim the excess paper. Sand the sides until they are smooth. Embellish your front cover as desired.

4. Punch holes and bind album
Punch two holes in the left side of the front cover. Using those holes as a guide, punch holes in the back cover and the rest of the pages. Add binder rings to bind your album.

Ribbon Detail
I love adding ribbon to all my albums. In this album, a simple loop acts as a makeshift chimney for my piggies' album home.

File Folder Album

Teaching scrapbooking is such a joy. I get to indulge my love of all things paper and glue, plus I get to travel to new places. A recent road trip to Seattle to teach at a scrapbooking convention was so enjoyable I wanted to document it via mini album. The idea of documenting conjured an image of file folders, so I made myself a file folder template and added maps, photos and embellishments to complete this mini road trip album.

Actual size: 5¾" × 4" (15cm × 10cm)

Supplies: Cardstock (WorldWin); patterned paper (KI Memories, Scenic Route); chipboard accents (Maya Road, Scenic Route); stickers (KI Memories); rub-ons (Karen Foster); brackets (American Crafts); mesh (Magic Mesh); dimensional gloss medium (Plaid); stamps (Inque Boutique); ink (Clearsnap, Tsukineko); embossing powder (Hampton Art); pen (American Crafts, Sakura)

Materials
* File Folder Template (page 124)
* cardstock (4 sheets)
* pen or pencil
* scissors or craft knife
* bone folder
* adhesive
* chalk ink

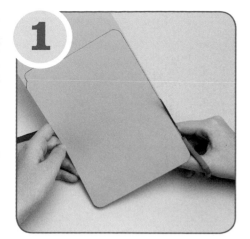

1

2

3

4

1. Trace template and cut folders
Enlarge and cut out the File Folder Template (on page 124). Trace it once onto each sheet of cardstock. Cut out the folders.

2. Fold and stack folders
Fold each file folder in half and set the crease with the bone folder. Then stack the folders, reversing the orientation so the tab on the first page is at the top, the tab on the second page is at the bottom, and so on.

3. Attach folders
Adhere the back (right) side of the first file folder to the front (left) of the second file folder. Then adhere the back (right) side of the second file folder to the front (left) of the third file folder. Do the same with the fourth folder. You should now have a book with a front and back cover and three inside pages.

4. Ink and embellish
Ink all edges of the folders with chalk ink. Then start embellishing!

Map It
When making an album about a road trip or vacation, don't forget the map! I printed this one from Google, but you can also cut pieces of one you used on your trip.

Accordion-Fold Album

A great birthday gift for a child is a nice memento of his or her special day. And what better place to record all the mementos than in a mini album? Knowing this challenged me to make a birthday book for my friend's young daughter. Using her favorite colors, I designed an accordion-fold album with a pocket for journaling tags on each page. You can also create this album as a special occasion card, or make shortened versions as favors for partygoers.

Actual size: 4" × 6" (10cm × 15cm)

Supplies: Cardstock; patterned paper and trim (Doodlebug); buttons (American Crafts, Doodlebug); ribbon (Creative Impressions, Making Memories, May Arts); chipboard shapes, clips (Making Memories); stickers (Doodlebug, KI Memories); rub-ons (Doodlebug, Heidi Grace); mesh (Magic Mesh); stamps (Inque Boutique); brad, photo turn, pins (Creative Impressions); chipboard tiles (Heidi Grace); ink (Clearsnap, Tsukineko); pen (Sakura)

Materials

Album
- cardstock (1 sheet)
- paper trimmer with scoring blade
- adhesive
- patterned paper (5 sheets)

Variation
- ribbon
- hole punch or Crop-A-Dile

1. Cut and fold cardstock

Cut the cardstock in half, so that you have two pieces measuring 6" × 12" (15cm × 30cm). Attach the scoring blade to your trimmer. Set one piece horizontally in the trimmer. Score the strip from the left edge at 4" (10cm) and at 8" (20cm). (See How to Score with a Trimmer on page 9 if needed.) You should now have three equal sections measuring 4" × 6" (10cm × 15cm). Repeat for the second piece of cardstock. Fold the strips accordion style (with mountain and valley folds).

2. Attach strips and cut paper

Open up the two strips so you can see the three sections. Adhere the left third of one strip of cardstock to the top of the right third of the other strip. You should now have one long strip with five sections. Next, cut five pieces of patterned paper measuring 5¾" × 3¾" (15cm × 10cm).

3. Attach paper to cardstock

Attach one piece of paper to the left-most section of cardstock. This is your cover. Attach the remaining pieces to the rest of the sections of cardstock. You can attach the papers completely to the cardstock, or you can make them into pockets, by adding thin lines of adhesive to the two sides and bottoms only. Ink the edges if desired.

Variation

As an alternative to my album, you can make your album vertical and allow it to hang. To do so, turn your album so the cover is at the top and the other sections hang down. Punch a hole in the top center of the cover and tie a loop of ribbon through the hole.

Easy Peasy Pockets

To make pockets easy to open, punch a half-circle at the top, using the hole punch. To make handy (and cute!) tags, attach ribbon or trim to the tops.

Album Technique

Embossed Cover

Growing up, I loved family camping trips—exploring new places far from noisy cities. I still love camping in the great outdoors. Brent, Zoey, Angus and I hike up mountains, swim in quiet lakes, eat fresh fish and sigh in awe at all the wondrous sights. To capture a glimpse of these places around British Columbia, I created this spiral-bound album, complete with inked and embossed cover techniques to bring out the rustic outdoor theme. This technique lends itself to lots of themes! The clear embossing will bring out the color of any album cover; try it on colored cardstock or patterned paper. Just switch the stamps to match your theme, then let your creativity show through.

Actual size: 6" × 6" (15cm × 15cm)

Supplies: Binding materials (Bind-it-All); cardstock; patterned paper (Scenic Route); letter stickers (American Crafts, Doodlebug); stamps (Gel-a-Tins); buttons (Creative Imaginations, other); acrylic paint (Ranger); ink (Tsukineko); pens (Sakura, Sanford, Uni-ball)

Materials

chipboard album
rubber stamp
watermark ink
clear embossing powder
heat gun
walnut ink
paper towel

1. Stamp image onto cover
Tap your stamp into the watermark ink, then stamp onto the album cover. To get a clean image, avoid rocking the stamp.

2. Add embossing powder
Quickly cover the stamped image completely with clear embossing powder. Dump the excess powder back into the container.

3. Melt embossing powder
Turn on the heat gun and run it evenly over the embossing powder until the entire image melts and becomes shiny. Be careful not to concentrate the heat in any one place for too long.

4. Apply walnut ink
Rub the walnut ink over the entire cover, including the embossed image. Wipe away the ink from the embossed image, and let the ink on the chipboard dry. The original color of the chipboard will show through the embossed letters.

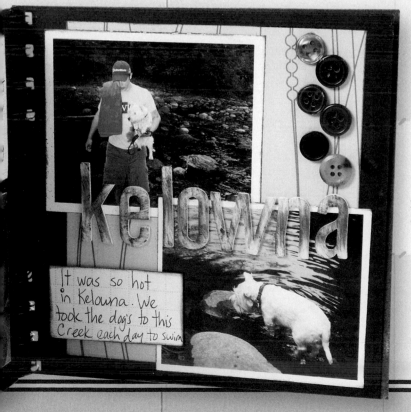

Color: Rubbing It In
Adding rustic-looking color to foam letters is easy! Simply rub colored pencils or paint over the foam.

Star Album

I enjoy experimenting with different shapes for scrapping projects, so a star mini album was definitely on my must-try list. I also wanted to dedicate a book to my father— one that was as unique, eye-catching and special as he is. So I created this star-shaped album for my star of a Dad to show him how much he means to me. With some masculine-looking papers, a little machine stitching and journaling from the heart, it truly shines as a mini album tribute.

MY DAD

my hero

Dad too

Materials
* cardstock (1 sheet)
* Large, Medium and Small Star templates (page 125)
* pen or pencil
* patterned paper (5 sheets)
* craft knife
* scissors (optional)
* adhesive
* sewing machine or needle and thread
* hole punch or Crop-A-Dile
* large eyelet
* eyelet setter and craft hammer or Crop-A-Dile
* binder ring (1½" [4cm])

Actual size: 7" × 7" (18cm 18cm)

Supplies: Cardstock (Bazzill, WorldWin); patterned paper (BasicGrey); letter stickers (American Crafts); eyelets (Provo Craft); fibers (Fiber Scraps); stamps (Close to My Heart, Gel-a-Tins, My Sentiments Exactly, Purple Onion); ink (Close to My Heart); adhesive (Beacon, Glue Dots, Xyron)

1. Trace and cut out stars

Photocopy and cut out the Large, Medium and Small Star templates (on page 125). Trace the Large Star five times onto cardstock. Trace the Large Star four times onto patterned paper. Trace the Medium Star five times onto patterned paper. Cut out all the stars. Then cut out the interior star on the Small Star Template using the craft knife. Trace it onto patterned paper and cut it out.

2. Stitch stars together

Stack a medium paper star on top of each large cardstock star (there are five); attach each one with just a dot of adhesive. Using a sewing machine (or a needle and thread if you prefer), stitch around the medium star near the edges. (Neatness doesn't count!) Then, stitch near the edges of the large patterned paper stars. Finally, stitch the small star outline to one of the completed large/medium stars. This star will be your cover.

3. Punch holes in pages

Pair the 10 large stars—one cardstock star (with medium star attached) and one patterned paper star. Adhere them back to back. You should now have five double-sided stars. Embellish your stars. Punch a hole in the top point of the cover star. Using the cover as a guide, mark and punch holes at the tops of the other pages.

4. Add eyelets

Set one large eyelet into each of the holes. Thread the binder ring through the holes. It's important to use a 1½" (4cm) binder ring so the points of the stars will easily pass through the ring without bending.

Texturize

Use a zigzag stitch in a contrasting color to sew your stars to create a patterned, textured look.

Library Pocket Album

The idea for this little flip book came to mind while talking with a young friend about her favorite foods. Our conversation elicited thoughts about other favorite things, enough to fill a mini album. To give this personal collection a unique and funky style, I gave each page a different look. To unify the mismatched pages, I added library pockets I designed myself to the pages. Mini library cards listing all Dasha's favorite things hide inside the pockets. The finished book is colorful, cute and cheerful, just like Dasha, and the library-inspired album is perfect for holding lots of information.

Actual size: 5" × 3½" (13 cm × 9cm)

Supplies: Cardstock (WorldWin); frames, patterned paper (Bam Pop); rub-ons, stickers (American Crafts, Arctic Frog, Doodlebug, KI Memories, Scenic Route, SEI); library card stamp (Close to My Heart); ribbon (Creative Impressions, Hobby Lobby, May Arts); dimensional gloss medium (Sakura); ink (Clearsnap, Tsukineko)

Materials
* cardstock (2 sheets)
* patterned paper (heavy-weight, 3 sheets)
* Library Pocket and Library Tag templates (page 125)
* pen or pencil
* scissors or craft knife
* chalk ink (optional)
* bone folder
* adhesive
* hole punch or Crop-A-Dile
* binder rings (2)
* large die-cuts (optional)

1. Trace and cut out templates
Photocopy and cut out the Library Pocket and Library Tag templates (on page 125). Trace the Pocket Template six times onto cardstock. Trace the Tag Template 14 times onto patterned paper. Cut out the shapes. Ink the edges, if desired.

2. Fold library pockets
Fold the library pockets in half as noted by the dashed line on the template. Then fold over the two sides as noted by the dotted lines on the template. Set the creases with a bone folder. Adhere the sides down to create pockets.

3. Pair tags and punch holes
Adhere two tags together to create one page. Repeat with the remaining tags. You should now have seven tag-shaped pages. Next, stack the tags and punch a hole in the top and bottom left corners (if the shortest edge faces right). Insert binder rings through the holes.

4. Attach library pockets to pages
Attach the six library pockets to one side of each inside tag. (The remaining tag is your cover page.) Make sure the pocket side is facing up. You can add large die-cuts as additional pages to create a more eclectic look.

Be Innovative!
Think of innovative ways to bind your album, like using zip ties or colored twist ties.

Envelope Pocket Album

Fernbank, my parents' country home, is dear to my heart and soothes my soul. Located in the lake district of Victoria, British Columbia, it is 10 acres of heaven. Large ponds attract water fowl and birds of all types, and the surrounding forest is home to beautiful wildlife including black-tailed deer, quail and squirrels, with occasional visits from cougars and bears. To capture the hidden treasure of this beautiful place, I crafted a mini album using envelopes as pockets for hiding away photo gems. Create an envelope album like mine to tuck away the special treasures of your own heart.

Actual size: 5½" × 4½" (14cm × 11cm)

Supplies: Binding materials (Bind-it-All); cardstock; patterned paper (Scenic Route); letter stickers (American Crafts); ribbon, rickrack (American Crafts, Creative Impressions); buttons (Creative Imaginations); dimensional gloss medium (Ranger); paint (DecoArt); ink (Clearsnap); pen (Sakura)

Materials
* chipboard (1 sheet)
* paper trimmer or scissors
* A2 envelopes (4)
* patterned paper (2 sheets)
* adhesive
* corner rounder
* chalk ink (optional)
* Bind-it-All machine or hole punch and binding materials (binder rings, ribbon, etc.)

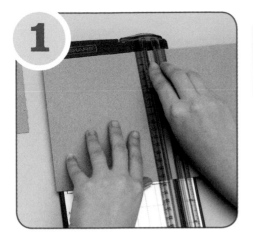

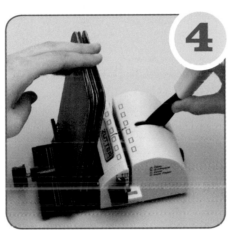

1. Cut out chipboard covers

Cut two pieces of chipboard to 5½" × 4½" (14cm × 11cm). (If your envelope size varies from mine, then cut your covers to the size of your envelopes.)

2. Seal and cut edges of envelopes

Seal the envelopes and turn them all flap side up. Then cut off ¼" (6mm) from the right side of each envelope. Your envelopes should now each have one open end, creating pockets.

3. Attach paper and round corners

Cut eight sheets of patterned paper to 5½" × 4½" (14 cm × 11cm). Attach paper to both sides of each envelope. Use the corner rounder to round the two corners on the open ends of the envelopes. Round one short edge of each chipboard cover as well. Ink the edges, if desired.

4. Bind pages

Stack the envelopes so that all the open ends are facing to the right. Place the stack between the chipboard covers and make sure all the rounded edges are facing the same way. Bind the stack using the Bind-it-All machine. Alternatively, you can punch holes in each page and bind with ribbon or binder rings.

Not-So-Empty Pockets

You can insert photos or memorabilia into your envelope pockets, or you can fill them with homemade tags. To create tags, cut cardstock to 5¼" × 4¼" (14cm × 11cm) and attach a loop of ribbon to the side.

Album Technique

Faux Epoxy Letters

As a lover of all things animal, I enjoy visiting zoos. Wild beasts inspired me to unleash my "wild" side to make this book featuring my zoo encounters. Thinking basic, natural and rough, I used scraps of chipboard and cardboard backing, fabric scraps, and bits and pieces of this and that to fashion this funky, tabbed album. I left edges natural, varied the size and shape of the pages, and doodled with several paints and inks, using "messy" techniques on the cover like these cool painted faux epoxy letters. Try making your own anytime you feel like going wild!

Actual size: 4½" × 6" (11cm × 15cm)

Supplies: Patterned paper (KI Memories, Scenic Route); chipboard letters (Zsiage); ribbon (American Crafts); sticker accents (KI Memories); labels (Dymo); dimensional gloss medium (Sakura); paint (DecoArt, Ranger); ink (Close to My Heart); pens (Bic, Sakura, Uni-ball); Misc: fabric, recipe cards

Materials

chipboard letters
sanding sponge (optional)
sponge brush
acrylic paint (2 colors)
dimensional gloss medium
needle (optional)

1. Brush on first paint color
Brush a coat of the darker paint color on each chipboard letter. No need to be even! If you don't have plain chipboard letters, you can use finished ones. Just sand down the finish a bit, then add a thick coat of paint.

2. Add second paint color
Brush on random strokes of the lighter paint color. Again, no need to be neat or even. If you want your colors to blend, make sure you brush on the second color before the first color dries. Allow all the paint to dry.

3. Coat with gloss medium
Add a thick coat of clear dimensional gloss medium to the surface of each painted letter. If you find air bubbles, simply pop them with a needle. Allow the dimensional gloss medium to dry completely (at least four hours) before attaching the letters to your album cover.

Play Tag

Making your own playful journaling tags is simple! Use a large circle or square punch (at least 2" [5cm] wide) to cut out shapes from lined paper. Then doodle around the edges to complete.

zebra

gorilla

Who could Resist this guys cute face?

This beautiful gorilla was one of our favorites. We took so many photos of her.

polar bear

rhino

monkey

Ribbon-Tied Accordion Album

Our darling cat, Gracie, is an unusual feline. When she plays with our other pets, she forgets she's a cat. Watching her play makes me think of storybook cats—and inspired this storybook-style mini album. I created accordion-fold pages held in place by sturdy chipboard covers. And I added a wrap-around ribbon to give an unusual touch to this book about my unusual cat.

Actual size: 4½" × 4½" (11cm × 11cm)

Supplies: Patterned paper, tabs (SEI); ribbon (May Arts); stickers (Doodlebug, Paper Studio); labels (Dymo); ink (Clearsnap, Tsukineko); pen (Sakura); adhesive (Beacon)

Materials
❋ chipboard (1 sheet)
❋ patterned paper (1 sheet)
❋ paper trimmer with scoring blade
❋ adhesive
❋ scissors
❋ cardstock (1 sheet)
❋ ribbon (1 piece, 21" [53cm])

1. Cut chipboard

Cut two squares of chipboard measuring 4½" × 4½" (11cm × 11cm). Cut two sqaures of patterned paper measuring 6" × 6" (15cm × 15cm). These sqaures will be used for your front and back covers.

2. Attach chipboard and paper squares

Adhere each chipboard square to the center of the wrong side of a paper square. Snip the four corners off the paper. Then fold over the sides and adhere them to the chipboard. Set the covers aside.

3. Cut cardstock into strips

Cut the sheet of cardstock into three 4" × 12" (10cm × 30cm) strips.

4. Score and fold cardstock

Attach the scoring blade to your trimmer. Set a strip of cardstock horizontally in the trimmer. Score the strip from the left edge at 4" (10cm) across and at 8" (20cm). (See How to Score with a Trimmer on page 9 if needed.) Bend the cardstock along the score lines.

5. Attach strips of cardstock

Adhere the three strips together. Start by attaching the right third of one strip to the left third of another. Then attach the right section of the new longer strip to the left third of the last strip of cardstock. Cut off the very last section. You should now have one long strip of cardstock with six sections. Bend the strip into an accordion fold (with mountain and valley folds). Set aside.

6. Adhere ribbon to cover

Lay the front cover piece face down. Attach the piece of ribbon across the middle of the cover piece, leaving about 6" (15cm) hanging off the left side of the cover and the remaining ribbon hanging off the right side. If your ribbon is single-sided, attach it right side down.

7. Attach pages to covers

Bend the strip of cardstock into an accordion fold (with mountain and valley folds). Start with a valley fold, then fold up into a mountain fold, down to a valley, up to mountain and back down to a valley fold. Attach the back sides of the first and last sections to the insides of the front and back covers.

All Tied Up

To close your album, fold up your accordion. Wrap the longer piece of ribbon around the back. Tie the ends together in a pretty bow.

"Tab" by Cat

Including tabs is a great way to add dimension and embellishment without adding much bulk to a page. I used tabs that match my cat-themed papers, but you can punch your own tabs or cut tabs out of a notebook divider. Use a label maker to add to the office-supply look.

Embellishment Alternative

Embellishments add detail and that perfect final touch to any mini album. Of course, you can buy an assortment of great items at your local store, but it's fun to make your own or use "alternative" items as embellishments. Give these a try!

❋ Venture outside and collect sticks, pebbles, sand or dried leaves to add to your book.
❋ Keep the tags that come on new clothes—many of them are very colorful and give a cool look when added to your pages.
❋ Keep receipts, movie ticket stubs, brochures, hotel room keys, etc. —these little tidbits of memorabilia add a unique and personal touch.
❋ Create your own buttons or other small accents using air-dry or polymer clay.
❋ Instead of using ribbon, cut up strips of fabric and tie them to the spine of your book.
❋ Cover stickers, titles, photos or chipboard with dimensional gloss medium like Glossy Accents (by Ranger) to create shiny, epoxy stickers.
❋ Go vintage! Take a trip to a flea market or thrift store and look for small treasures.
❋ Many tourist places have coin machines where you can put a penny in, and it flattens the penny and imprints an image. These make great additions to mini travel albums.

Flower Album

I wanted to showcase some special sister bonds in a unique way. While pondering this idea, I rested my eyes on a vase of fresh flowers. Inspiration struck again, giving me a way to combine a love of flowers, my sister, my nieces, and, of course, scrapping. I took the latest "Jess original" to the next level and involved a few materials from the hardware store. But don't let that turn you off! With tons of flower power, this girly sister creation is feminine to its core.

Actual size: 13" × 13" (33cm × 33cm)

Supplies: Frames, labels, patterned paper, tabs (SEI); rub-ons, stickers (American Crafts, SEI); rhinestones (Me & My Big Ideas); buttons (American Crafts, Doodlebug); ribbon (Creative Impressions); chipboard shapes, transparent flowers (Heidi Swapp); glitter glue, glossy topcoat (Ranger); paint pen (Marvy)

Materials
* Petal and Circle templates (page 124)
* chipboard (2 sheets)
* patterned paper (2 sheets)
* pen or pencil
* scissors or craft knife
* sewing machine and thread (optional)
* adhesive
* sanding sponge
* paper piercer
* screw (½" [1cm] or shorter)
* washer (to fit screw)
* nut (to fit screw)
* hole punch (optional)
* screwdriver

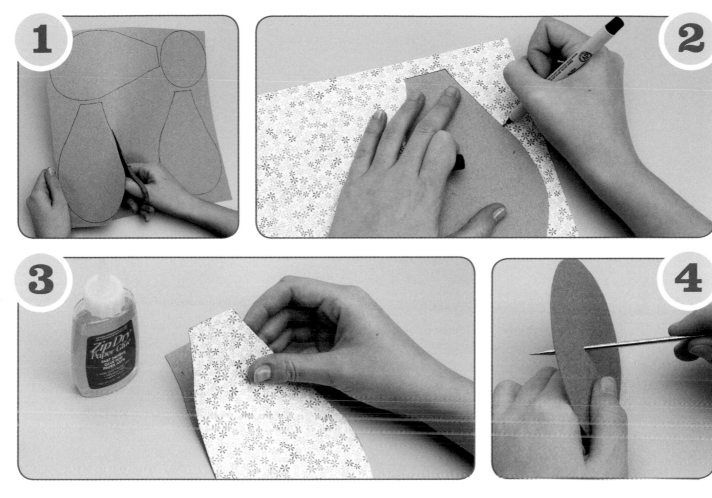

1. Trace templates and cut out chipboard
Photocopy and cut out the Petal Template and Circle Template (on page 124).
Trace the Petal Template five times onto chipboard. Trace the Circle Template
onto chipboard once. Cut out all six shapes.

2. Cut out paper pieces
Trace the chipboard petals onto patterned paper. Trace the chipboard circle
onto patterned paper. Cut out all six shapes. If you want to add machine
stitching to the patterned paper petals, do it now. Set the Circle Template and
the circle pieces aside.

3. Attach chipboard and paper pieces
Attach all the paper petals to the chipboard petals with adhesive. Gently sand
all the edges.

4. Poke hole in chipboard circle
Use a paper piercer to poke a hole in the center of the chipboard circle. Use
the dot in the Circle Template as a guide, if needed.

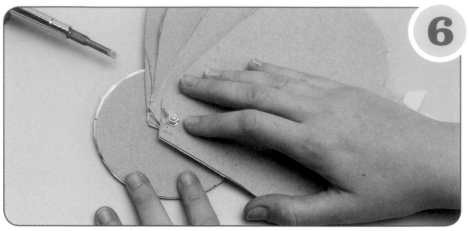

5. Poke holes in petals

Stack all the petals together and place them so that the bases of the petals overlap the hole in the circle. Use the paper piercer to poke a hole in each petal, using the hole in the circle as a guide. Check to see that all the holes line up correctly.

6. Screw petals and circle together

Stack the circle and petals with the holes aligned. Insert the screw from the front to the back of the stack. (If you find your screw is too difficult to insert, then punch over the pierced holes with a 1/16" [2mm] hole punch.) Add the washer to the end of the screw and then add the nut, and tighten everything with the screwdriver. Be careful not to tighten too much; you want to be able to move the petals freely.

7. Cover circle with paper

Add photos and embellish the front of your petals. Then adhere the paper circle over the top of the chipboard circle, covering the screw. Add your title, and your flower is ready to go!

Flat into Fabulous

Choose embellishments that are flat—no thicker than a small button—to keep the petals moving freely. Keep in mind that flat doesn't mean boring! Use acrylic shapes, machine stitching, chipboard and ribbon scraps to add color, texture and a little dimension.

Got Her in My Pockets

Even without square pages, you can still create pockets for housing extra photos or sweet sentiments. All you have to do is attach a photo with just a line of adhesive on three of the sides, leaving the fourth side open.

Add Some Bling!

With their soft, cushy texture, foam letters are a fabulous addition to feminine albums. To add some girly bling, apply a bit of glitter glue to the tops of letters and seal them with clear dimensional gloss medium. Use different styles of letters to give a sweet cover a funky edge.

Matchbook Album

Some people can always put a smile on your face. Randi, my friend and co-worker, is such a person. I made this little album for her using lively portraits to capture all her many faces. To hold the photos, I designed a matchbook album, which may appear difficult but is easy to assemble. Plus, its folded cover hiding the pages inside makes it a great gift. Of course, I couldn't stop at "ordinary" pages, so I added pull-out accordion-fold pages inside to add some flair.

Actual size: 4¼" × 5½" (11cm × 14cm)

Supplies: Cardstock; patterned paper (Cosmo Cricket); chipboard letters (BasicGrey); chipboard shapes (Making Memories); rhinestones (Heidi Swapp); flowers (Creative Imaginations, Prima); brads (Karen Foster, Making Memories); dimensional glitter glue (Ranger); inks (Clearsnap, Fiber Scraps); pen (Sakura)

Materials
* paper trimmer with scoring blade
* patterned paper (heavy-weight, 1 sheet cut to 4¼" × 12" [11cm × 30cm])
* cardstock (1 sheet)
* scissors (optional)
* pen or pencil
* paper piercer
* brads (2)
* adhesive

1. Score and fold patterned paper

Attach the scoring blade to your trimmer. Set the patterned paper strip in the trimmer horizontally and score it three times from the left edge: at 1" (3cm), at 6½" (17cm) and at 7" (18cm). (See How to Score with a Trimmer on page 9 if needed.) Bend at the score marks and fold the strip so it closes like a matchbook.

2. Cut and score cardstock

Cut your solid cardstock into three strips, each measuring 4" × 12" (10cm × 30cm). Set one strip horizontally in the trimmer (the scoring blade should still be attached). Score the strip from the left edge at 5½" (14cm) and at 9¾" (25cm). Score the second and third strips at 4¼" (11cm) and at 8½"(22cm).

3. Cut off end of strip

Cut the smallest section off the end of the first strip.

4. Insert first strip into matchbook

Starting with the first strip, insert the largest section (measuring 4" × 5½" [10cm × 14 cm]) into the matchbook and center it under the small flap.

5. Insert brads to secure

Mark two holes on the front of the flap about 1" (3cm) from each side. Pierce the holes from the front of the flap through the cardstock and the back of the matchbook. Insert brads from the front of the flap through the back to secure the cardstock in place.

6. Attach second and third strips of cardstock

Lay the matchbook horizontally. Take the second strip of cardstock and attach the right-most section (measuring 4" × 4¼" [10cm × 11cm]) over the top of the left-most section (measuring 4" × 4¼" [10cm × 11cm]) of the strip secured in the matchbook. Take the third strip and attach it to the second strip in the same way. Fold the pages into an accordion (with mountain and valley folds), making sure that the four middle pages measure no wider than 4¼" (11cm). (The left-most page will be 3½" [9cm] wide.)

Thinner Than a Matchstick

To close the matchbook, flip over the cover and tuck it inside the flap. When embellishing your album, keep in mind that using lots of thick embellishments will keep the book from closing correctly. Felt shapes and thin metal or acrylic elements work well, as long as they are not placed in similar locations on each page. Keep in mind that the spine of the album is meant to hold only a stack of pages less than ½" (1cm) high.

Polaroid "Faux"tos

With their small, square size and built-in space for words, Polaroid pictures are perfect for mini albums! If you don't have a real Polaroid camera, you can fake the look. Open your photo in an image-editing software program. Resize it to 2¾" × 3¼" (7cm × 8cm). Print the photo onto white photo paper. Then cut out the photo leaving a thin border on three sides and a thicker border along the bottom. You can accomplish this same look with already-printed photos, too; just attach them to white cardstock and cut.

Sparkle and Shine

To make the faces in your portraits really shine, add a bit of glitter and gleam. I love to use glitter glue (like Ranger's) to add extra texture and color to simple felt flowers. You can also attach rhinestone brads or stickers to add some extra zing.

Mini Maze Album

These tiny maze albums are the perfect fit for capturing the twists, turns and unexpected moments of life. Learning the maze technique can be a bit challenging, but once you master it, I guarantee you'll find yourself hooked! Just one sheet of 12" × 12" (30cm × 30cm) paper provides plenty of pages and pockets, too. Bind your mini maze book with coils, or simply add a ribbon. Then "a-maze" all your friends with this clever technique! Are you up for the challenge?

Actual size: 3½" × 3½" (9cm × 9cm)

Supplies: Cardstock (WorldWin); patterned paper (Creative Imaginations, Making Memories, Scenic Route); binding materials (Bind-it-All); stickers (Making Memories, Paper Studio, Scenic Route); chipboard shapes (American Crafts, Making Memories, Scenic Route); ribbon (American Crafts); twine (Creative Impressions); labels (Dymo); ink (Clearsnap, Ranger, Tsukineko); pen (Sakura); adhesive (Beacon); Misc: fabric

Materials

Album
- ❋ paper trimmer with scoring blade
- ❋ cardstock (1 sheet)
- ❋ paper-clips (optional)
- ❋ adhesive
- ❋ small circle punch (optional)
- ❋ chipboard (1 sheet)
- ❋ patterned paper (1 sheet)
- ❋ scissors
- ❋ ribbon (19" [48cm])

Variation
- ❋ Bind-it-All machine
- ❋ Bind-it-All coils

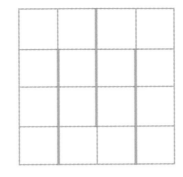

Scoring/Cutting Diagram
Gray lines indicate scoring.
Green lines indicate cutting.

1. Score cardstock
Attach the scoring blade to your trimmer. Score your sheet of cardstock from the left edge at 3" (8cm), 6" (15cm) and 9" (23cm). (See How to Score with a Trimmer on page 9 if needed.) Flip your cardstock 90 degrees. Score again at 3" (8cm), 6" (15cm) and 9" (23cm). Your sheet should have 16 boxes. (See diagram.)

2. Cut along scored lines
Replace the scoring blade with the cutting blade. Cut along the first scored line from the left side. Cut from bottom to top and stop before you've reached the last square. Do the same along the first scored line from the right. Then cut along the middle scored line but from top to bottom. (See diagram.)

3. Accordion-fold cardstock
Starting with one of the two end squares, fold the cardstock accordion style (with valley and mountain folds). The first and last squares are the covers. Two squares make one inside page. So, you should now have a book with front and back covers and seven inside pages. You can paper-clip each pair of squares to keep track of the pages as you work, if desired.

4. Make pockets, if desired
If you do not want your pages to become pockets, then adhere each pair of squares to make a solid page. To make pockets, begin by punching half-circles: Starting with the first inside page (the first pair of squares), punch a half-circle at the top of one square (not both together).

5. Finish punching pages
On the next page, punch a half-circle on the side (not the top). Then punch the next page on top, as you did in step 4. Repeat until you reach the last page. Once you're finished, you should see that pages with a fold on the side will have pockets that open at the top. Pages with a fold at the top or bottom will have pockets that open to the side.

Variation

If you have a Bind-it-All, you can make a spiral-bound album. Follow the directions above and on the previous page, but with these changes: At the end of step 2, cut off the first and last squares. When you fold your album, you'll end up with eight inside pages. After you create your chipboard cover pieces, cut out two squares of paper measuring 3⅛" (8cm); attach these to the unfinished sides of the covers. Skip steps 8 and 9 and bind your album to finish.

6. Adhere pocket pages
Close your pocket pages. Add just a thin line of adhesive to all open sides without a half-circle. When you're finished, set the pages aside.

7. Create covers
Cut two pieces of chipboard measuring 3¼" × 3¼" (8cm × 8cm). Cut two pieces of patterned paper measuring 4¼" × 4¼" (11cm × 11cm). Flip a paper square face down. Adhere the chipboard square to it. Snip off the corners of the paper, fold the sides over and adhere them to the chipboard. Repeat with the other paper and chipboard squares.

8. Add ribbon for binding
Lay your covers face down about ½" (1cm) apart. Lay your piece of ribbon (face down if it's single-sided) horizontally over the covers; center the ribbon on the covers. Be sure the center point of the piece of ribbon is between the two covers.

9. Adhere cardstock to covers
Finally, adhere the front and back covers of your cardstock album to the wrong sides of the chipboard covers.

Ribbon and Raffia

It's no secret that I am a big fan of ribbon scraps—they make great (and cute!) pull tabs for tags. But sometimes you need to think outside the ribbon box! Try adding twine or raffia to your tags to give a beach- or camping-themed album a more natural look.

Mini Album Theme Ideas

Love and beaches are just two of so many themes that you can turn into adorable albums! Whether you're looking for inspiration or want some gift ideas, use these themes to turn your homemade albums into memory art.

※ Graduation
※ Anniversary
※ College Years
※ Dreams and Hopes
※ New Year's Resolutions
※ Baby's Firsts
※ Baby Shower or Wedding Shower Advice
※ Honeymoon
※ Summer Fun
※ What I Wish For
※ Friends Forever

※ Never Thought I Would …
※ Our Hometown
※ To Do Before I Die
※ Wish Come True
※ Celebrating Me
※ Best Advice
※ Favorite Poems
※ People I Admire
※ I Want to Be …
※ Inspiration
※ Books I Love

reduce,
RECYCLE, REUSE

Making Mini Albums out of Everyday Items

With all the paper scraps we amass, scrapbookers may not be the best at being "green." But you can make the most of what you've got and reinvent everyday items into truly one-of-a-kind mini album masterpieces! Check out my paper lunch bag book on page 72 and my coffee cup album on page 86—just a few of the many innovative ways to display all kinds of memories. Come on: See how you can turn your own trash into treasure with these creative projects!

Coffee Filter Album

I'm blessed with a wonderful family. We aren't a large group but we are close and enjoy being in each other's company. During a recent visit with my parents, I watched as Dad prepared to brew his favorite beverage. Instant inspiration! I thought cone coffee filters (unused ones, of course!) would make a great mini album. They are an interesting shape for pages and have a ready-made pocket for holding journaling tags and extra photos. This uniquely shaped album is perfect for the individuality of every family.

Actual size: 5½" × 7½" (14cm × 19cm)

Supplies: Cardstock; patterned paper (Rusty Pickle); letter stickers (American Crafts); word stickers (Making Memories); chipboard tiles (Scenic Route); ribbon (Creative Impressions); rub-ons (BasicGrey); glossy topcoat (Ranger); watercolor pencils (Reeves); ink (Clearsnap); pen (Sakura); Misc: binder clip, fabric

Materials

Album
* cardstock (2 sheets)
* #4 cone coffee filters (4)
* adhesive
* scissors
* pen or pencil
* patterned paper (2 sheets)
* hole punch or Crop-A-Dile
* binder rings (2)

Tags
* cardstock (2 sheets)
* patterned paper (2 sheets)
* ribbon scraps (4)
* stapler

1. Stabilize filter with cardstock
Adhere a coffee filter to cardstock. Trim around the filter, leaving a small cardstock border (about ⅛" [3mm]). Repeat with the other three filters.

2. Trace shape onto paper
Trace a cardstock-backed coffee filter onto patterned paper. Cut out the filter shape, about ¼" (6mm) inside the traced line. Adhere the paper to the top of the cardstock-backed coffee filter. Repeat with the other four pages.

3. Punch holes and add rings
Embellish your album as desired. Then punch two holes along the vertical edge of your coffee-filter pages. Insert small binder rings to bind the album.

Create Filter-Shaped Tags
You can fill your coffee-filter pockets with additional photos or memorabilia. Or you can make custom-fit tags. Trace a coffee-filter page onto cardstock and cut it out about ¼" (6mm) inside the line. Trace that piece of cardstock onto patterned paper and cut that out about ⅛" (3mm) inside the line. Add photos and embellishments to the tags. Staple on ribbon scraps to finish.

Coffee Cup Sleeve Album

I am always looking for new and different media from which to create mini books, so I couldn't resist the urge to try coffee cup sleeves as unique pages. This is a short little book and quick to make. None of us really has too many things to confess, right? So, it doesn't require a lot of materials or time to put it together. The most difficult part is admitting to your imperfections, and the rest is a breeze.

Materials
* coffee cup sleeves (6)
* patterned paper (2 sheets)
* paper trimmer or scissors
* adhesive
* hole punch or Crop-A-Dile
* pen
* binder ring
* ribbon and rickrack
* scissors

Actual size: 5" × 2¾" (13cm × 7cm)

Supplies: Cardboard; cardstock; patterned paper (BasicGrey); chipboard letters and shapes, rub-ons (American Crafts); binder ring (Junkitz); clips, ribbon, rickrack (Creative Impressions); tags (Making Memories); ink (Clearsnap, Tsukineko); pens (American Crafts, Sakura)

1. Cut out patterned paper
Cut the patterned paper into 12 pieces of slightly differing sizes. (Most of mine are about 4¼" × 2¾" [11cm × 7cm].) The papers can be larger or smaller than the coffee cup sleeve to create an eclectic look.

2. Attach paper to sleeves
Adhere the paper pieces to both sides of the coffee cup sleeves. Embellish your pages as desired.

3. Mark and punch holes
Punch a hole in the top left corner of the cover page. Use that hole as a guide to mark holes for the other pages. Punch those holes as well.

4. Add ribbon to binder ring
Insert a binder ring into the holes to bind the album. Tie ribbon and rickrack pieces to the binder ring to embellish it. Your confession is over. Go out and enjoy the rest of the day!

"Realize" Your Book
Keep in mind that in a confessions book, the messier the better! This will make your book—and your confessions—seem more real. Handwrite your words. Gather items like candy wrappers and clothing tags to accompany photos. And attach miscellaneous embellishments like paper clips, colored staples, bulldog clips and loops of rickrack.

Corrugated Cardboard Album

This mini album feels rough and tough because the pages are made using corrugated cardboard cut from an IKEA box. It seemed an appropriate medium for a guy-themed book. The great thing about using cardboard is that you can cut it easily to any size you want. If you shop online like I do, it's always easy to find a vast amount of cardboard to use!

Materials

❋ corrugated cardboard
   (enough for four 6" × 6"
   [15cm × 15cm] pieces)
❋ scissors or utility knife
❋ hole punch or Crop-A-Dile
❋ ribbon (4 pieces, 5"
   [13cm] each)
❋ clean twig (about 6" [15cm])
❋ acrylic paint
❋ paintbrush

Actual size: 6" × 6" (15cm × 15cm)

Supplies: Patterned paper (Dude Designs); chipboard brackets and letters (American Crafts, BasicGrey); chipboard shapes (Making Memories); ribbon (Creative Impressions, May Arts); rub-ons, stickers (American Crafts, Doodlebug, Dude Designs, Junkitz, Scenic Route); labels (Around the Block); stamps (Gel-a-Tins); buttons (American Crafts); mesh (Magic Mesh); acrylic paint (Ranger); inks (Clearsnap, Tsukineko); pens (American Crafts, Sakura, Uni-ball); adhesive (Beacon)

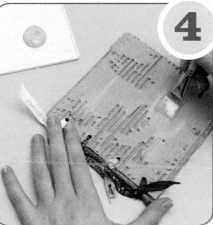

1. Cut cardboard

Cut the four pieces of corrugated cardboard to 6" × 6" (15cm × 15cm) using scissors or a utility knife. Tear the top layer of paper off the cardboard so it reveals pieces of the middle, ridged layer.

2. Punch holes and insert ribbon

Punch four evenly spaced holes down the left edge of one piece of cardboard. Use these holes as a guide to punch holes in the other pages. Stack the pages, then thread a piece of ribbon through each hole, leaving the pieces untied.

3. Tie twig to spine

Align the twig along the spine of the album. Take the piece of ribbon in the top hole. Wrap the left side of the ribbon over the stick then under and back to the left side. Wrap the right side over and under and back out to the right side. Tie the sides together. Repeat to bind the twig to the other three holes.

4. Paint cardboard pages

Randomly brush different colors of paint across each page to give it a funky, rough-and-tumble look.

Make It Masculine

Even scrapbooking can be masculine! Use cardboard scraps to create photo frames for your album. Then add other natural-looking or rough elements like mesh, brown cardstock, twine and metal.

Coaster Album

When I decided to document our recent vacation to Southern California, I remembered all the thrilling rollercoaster rides we enjoyed. So it seemed appropriate to use actual coasters as the base for this book. Plus, the round Mickey Mouse shape looks great against a square background. The result: a small mini album that can easily fit on a desk or shelf. I love sharing this delightful little book highlighting the excitement of our trip.

Materials

Album
* 5 chipboard coasters (3½" × 3½" [9cm × 9cm])
* patterned paper (2 sheets)
* paper trimmer (optional)
* scissors or craft knife
* adhesive
* sanding sponge
* hole punch or Crop-A-Dile
* ribbon pieces or binder rings (2)

Pockets
* patterned Aper (1 sheet)

Actual size: 3½" × 3½" (9cm × 9cm)

Supplies: Cardstock; patterned paper (Scenic Route); stickers (American Crafts); label (Dymo); binder ring (Junkitz); button (Doodlebug); glitter glaze (Li'l Davis); glass top coat (Plaid); ink (Clearsnap, Fiber Scraps, Ranger); stamps (Close to My Heart); pen (American Crafts, Sakura, Sanford)

1. Cut out patterned paper
Cut 10 pieces of patterned paper measuring 3½" × 3½" (9cm × 9cm). (If your coasters are larger than mine, increase the size of the squares to match the size of the coasters.)

2. Attach paper to coasters
Attach a paper square to one side of a coaster. Trim the edges and corners. Add paper to the other side and trim the edges. Repeat with the remaining coasters.

3. Sand edges and punch holes
Sand all the edges of your coasters. Then punch two holes along the left edge of your cover piece, about 1" (3cm) from the top and bottom. Use these holes as a guide to punch holes in the other pages.

4. Bind album
Stack your pages with the holes aligned. Insert a piece of ribbon in both holes and tie. You can bind your album with binder rings instead, if you prefer.

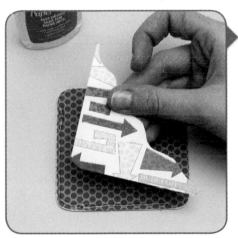

Cut Triangular Pockets
Cut a square of patterned paper to 3½" × 3½" (9cm × 9cm). Then cut the square in half on the diagonal. You can cut the diagonal in a wavy pattern if you like. Attach it to the page along the straight edges. Trim the corners.

Fake Your Memorabilia
If you don't have memorabilia to fill pockets, fake it! I made my own by heat embossing this stamped ticket image.

Lunch Bag Recipe Book

What's better suited for a book full of meal ideas than bags meant to hold lunch? This jam-packed album is made of brown paper lunch bags folded and opened at both ends. Paper bag albums are so much fun to make, and they're really easy! This album holds my most favorite and cherished family recipes. The open ends of the bags are ready-made pockets to hold all the recipes, and the best thing is that I can easily add more recipes to the pockets over time.

Actual size: 5½" × 5½" (14cm × 14cm)

Supplies: Cardstock; patterned paper (Tada Creative); ribbon (Creative Impressions); stickers (American Crafts, Doodlebug); clips (Making Memories); clear accents (Robin's Nest); mesh (Magic Mesh); tabs (Hot off the Press); inks (Clearsnap, Tsukineko); pens (Sakura, Uni-ball); acrylic paint (DecoArt, Ranger); 3D Crystal Lacquer (Sakura)

Materials
* 4 paper lunch bags
* paper trimmer or scissors
* large tapestry needle
* ribbon (about ⅛" [3mm] wide and 10" [25cm] long)

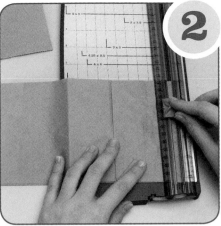

1. Stack and arrange bags

Stack the paper bags horizontally, flaps up, and alternate the ends (i.e., one bag with the closed end to the left, the next bag with the closed end to the right, etc.). The bottom bag should have the closed end on the left.

2. Trim ends

Trim about ¼" [6mm] off the edges of the closed ends of the top three bags.

3. Fold bags

Stack the bags once more and fold the stack in half to create a book with square pages. The album should now have a pocket on every page except for the cover.

4. Begin binding album

Thread the needle with the ribbon. Open your stack of bags and make sure the inside is facing up. In the fold, poke your needle about 1" (3cm) from the top. Thread the ribbon through to the outside of the book, leaving about 2½" (6cm) of ribbon inside.

5. Finish binding

Flip the book over. Your needle should now be on the outside spine of the album. Insert your needle about 1" (3cm) from the bottom of the album. On the inside of the album, tie the ribbon ends together in a knot.

Doodlebug

For a personalized, whimsical feel for a paper bag album, add hand-drawn pictures.

Playing Card Album

Quick, what comes to mind when you think Vegas? You guessed it: cards! I wanted a memento of our Vegas trip that would capture the essence of this glittering city, famous for games. So the cards and their box became my mini album. I used six cards as pages, covering them on both sides with photos, cuttings from tourist brochures, embellishments and quotes. I glued a plastic casino chip to the painted box front to complete this perfect vacation reminder.

Actual size: Box is 2½" × 3½" (6cm × 9cm)

Supplies: Patterned paper (Sassafras Lass); stickers (Adornit, American Crafts, Making Memories); rub-ons (Karen Foster, Scenic Route); mesh (Magic Mesh); inks (Clearsnap); pens (Sakura, Uni-ball); adhesive (Beacon)

Materials
* box of playing cards
* paintbrush
* white gesso
* patterned paper (2 sheets)
* paper trimmer or scissors
* chalk ink
* corner rounder (optional)
* adhesive
* Crop-A-Dile or hole punch
* metal beaded cord
* makeup sponge

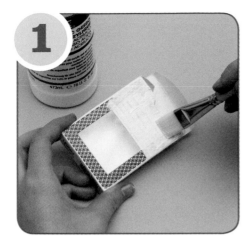

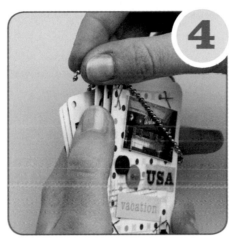

1. Paint gesso on box

Remove the cards from the box and choose six for the pages of the album. Set the cards aside. Paint the box with three layers of gesso and let it dry.

2. Cut patterned paper

Cut the patterned paper into 16 rectangles smaller than the playing cards (no bigger than 2¼" × 3¼" [6cm × 8cm]). Ink the edges and round the corners, if desired.

3. Embellish pages

Embellish the cards with tiny photos, pieces of tickets and brochures, stickers, rub-ons, etc. In order to be able to fit the album inside the box, make sure embellishments are thin and don't hang off the edges of the cards.

4. Punch holes and bind

Punch a hole in the top left corner of your first page. (You'll get the easiest punch with the Crop-A-Dile.) Use this hole as a guide to punch the rest of the pages. Insert the metal beaded cord into the hole to hold the pages together.

5. Ink box and embellish

Use the makeup sponge to apply chalk ink along the edges and sides of the card box. Add stickers and embellishments, then insert your album.

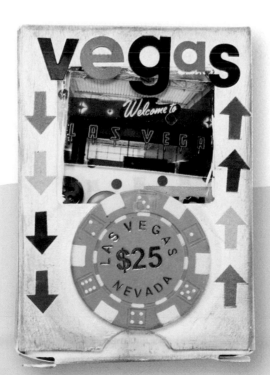

Peek-a-Boo

If your card box has a window, keep this in mind as you embellish your first album page. For example, place a photo like this one so that it shows through the window.

Clear Badge Album

Betcha didn't know

Everyone has a few secrets, sometimes not even revealed to family or friends. I had been toying with the idea of sharing some idiosyncrasies in a mini album when I came across Canadian paper. These patterns provided the perfect background for an album about me, not-so-subtly sharing I am a proud Canadian. And I had fun sharing a few secrets. When my mother read this little book, she was surprised about some of the things I revealed. "You're right!" she exclaimed. "I didn't know."

Materials
- clear badges (5)
- patterned paper (1 sheet, double-sided)
- paper trimmer or scissors
- chalk ink
- Crop-A-Dile
- ribbon (4 pieces)

Actual size: 4¼" × 4¼" (11cm × 11cm)

Supplies: Patterned paper (Rusty Pickle, Scenic Route); rub-ons, stickers (Luxe); ribbons (Creative Impressions, May Arts); watercolor pencils (Reeves); inks (Close to My Heart, Clearsnap); pen (Sakura)

1. Cut out patterned paper
Cut five pieces of patterned paper to 3½" × 4" (9cm × 10cm). Ink the edges of your pages.

2. Punch holes in badges
Remove any straps from the badges. Orient a badge so that the pocket is face down. Mark four holes along the pocket edge—two at the top and two at the bottom, each set about an inch apart. Punch the holes and use these as a guide to punch holes in the other badges.

3. Embellish and insert pages
Add photos and embellishments to both sides of your paper pages. Slip each page inside the badge pockets.

4. Bind album with ribbon
Insert ribbons and fabric scraps into the holes and tie them to bind your album.

All About Embellishing

It's important to stick with flat embellishments like rub-ons for your pages so that they fit inside the badge pockets. But if you'd like to add dimensional embellishments (which I admit is hard to resist!) simply attach them to the outsides of the badges. Loosen your ribbon binding as needed so that your pages turn easily.

Laminated Pouch Album

I had a package of business-card-sized laminating pouches on my desk for a while (don't ask me why) and the more I looked at them, the more I wanted to make a mini book with them (of course!). Making sure to keep the pages as flat as possible, I used an iron to seal the pouches. The end result is a tiny album perfect to carry in a purse. It won't get bent or wrinkled, and it's even waterproof!

Materials

- patterned paper (1 sheet, double-sided)
- paper trimmer or scissors
- laminating pouches (6)
- ironing board
- iron
- towel
- laminating machine (optional)
- paper piercer
- brad

Actual size: 3¾" × 2¼" (10cm × 6cm)

Supplies: Patterned paper (Rusty Pickle); rub-ons, stickers (Adornit, American Crafts, Arctic Frog, Doodlebug, Paper Studio, Pebbles); stamps (Gel-a-Tins); watercolor pencils (Reeves); inks (Clearsnap, Tsukineko); pen (Sakura)

1. Cut out pages and embellish
Cut six pieces of patterned paper to 3½" × 2" (9cm × 5cm). Add photos and embellishments to your pages. Keep your embellishments as flat as possible; each page should be no thicker than two photos stacked together.

2. Seal pouches with iron
Place a paper page inside a laminating pouch. Place the pouch on an ironing board and lay a towel on top of the pouch. Iron on high heat for about 20 seconds. (You can also put the pouches through a laminator instead.) Repeat with the other five pouches.

3. Poke holes in pages
Using the paper piercer, poke a hole through the upper left corner of the cover page. Use this hole as a guide for marking and poking holes in the other pages.

4. Insert brad
Insert the brad through the hole, from front to back, and bend the prongs to secure.

Binding with Brads
Brads make easy binding for thin albums that open like a fan, like this one. And brads keep your album neatly stacked for storing in your purse. Try using a brad to bind the Clear Badge Album on page 76, too. But if brads aren't your thing, you can punch holes and insert a binder ring, metal bead chain or ribbon instead.

CD Album

Covered CDs make sturdy album pages. And who doesn't have a few old CDs lying around? Making a mini album with CDs is a great way to clean up the office! We visited Kauai to attend a wedding, so using CDs, which mimic the circular shape of wedding bands, seemed appropriate for highlighting our priceless Kauai memories. You'll want to make sure you have a Crop-A-Dile on hand for this one; it punches tough holes with ease!

Actual size: 4¼" (11cm) in diameter

Supplies: Chipboard circles (Scenic Route); patterned paper (Making Memories, Rusty Pickle); chipboard letters (American Crafts); stickers (Arctic Frog, Me & My Big Ideas); rub-ons (Karen Foster); decorative tape (Making Memories); pens (Sakura, Uni-ball); adhesive (Beacon); Misc: CDs, fabric strips, sanding sponge

Materials

* CDs (5)
* sanding sponge
* patterned paper (3 sheets)
* paper trimmer (optional)
* strong liquid glue (like Zip Dry)
* scissors
* Crop-A-Dile
* binder ring

1. Sand CDs
Sand both sides of each CD. This will help the adhesive stick to them.

2. Cut out patterned paper
Cut 10 squares of patterned paper to 4¾" × 4¾" (12cm × 12cm).

3. Glue paper to CDs
Glue paper squares onto both sides of the CDs. Trim off the excess paper around the edges. Once all the CDs are covered, sand all the edges until they are smooth.

4. Punch holes and bind
Using the Crop-A-Dile, punch a hole near the edge of the cover CD. Use this hole as a guide to punch holes in the other CDs. Insert a binder ring.

Write in White

White paint pens are perfect for writing on photos. Their ink won't smudge on a photo's slick surface. And white, hand-drawn borders lend a sweet touch to albums. My favorite white pens are Sharpie's paint pens and Uni-ball's Signo.

Vintage Record Album

I love making trips to local thrift stores to see what mini album treasures I can discover. On one recent trip, I found a pile of old records, along with some awesome New Kids on the Block shoelaces, and I immediately had an idea for an '80s-themed album. I had tons of fun reminiscing about my childhood while I put it all together.

Materials
* 6¾" (17cm) records (4)
* patterned paper (4 sheets)
* circle cutter or round object 6" (15cm) wide
* pen
* scissors
* strong liquid glue (like Zip Dry)
* transparency
* paint pen
* Crop-A-Dile
* binder rings (2)
* ribbon pieces

Actual size: 6¾" (17cm) in diameter

Supplies: Die-cut shapes, patterned paper (Daisy D's); ribbon (Jo-Ann's); rickrack (Creative Impressions); chipboard letters, stickers (American Crafts); rhinestones (Me & My Big Ideas); buttons (Creative Imaginations); mesh (Magic Mesh); ink (Clearsnap); paint (Ranger); paint pen (Marvy, Sakura)

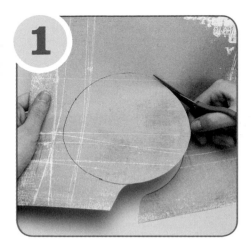

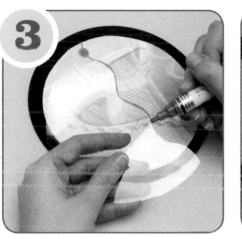

1. Cut paper circles

Cut eight circles with a 6" (15cm) diameter. If you don't have a circle cutter, you can trace anything round that is the right size, like a plate or a box lid.

2. Glue paper to records

Glue the paper circles to both sides of the records.

3. Make transparency pockets

Cut a 6" (15cm) circle out of the transparency. Then cut the circle in half. You can cut in a wavy pattern if you like. Ink the top edge of one half-circle with the colored paint pen. Apply a thin line of glue to the circular edge of the transparency and attach it to a record.

4. Punch holes

Punch two holes, about 1" (3cm) apart, in the cover record using the Crop-A-Dile. Use these holes as a guide to punch holes in the other records. Insert binder rings and tie ribbons and fabric to them.

Inspire Nostalgia

Scour thrift stores for memorabilia. I found old shoelaces to use as ribbon, and cut pieces of old book covers to act as embellishments. Play up the theme with decade-inspired paper like the bright-colored funky patterns I used.

Child's Board Book Album

Thrift stores hold more hidden treasures than just records! On another recent thrift store adventure, I came across a well-worn child's board book. I decided it would make an excellent sturdy base for a mini scrapbook. My two pet dogs agreed with me, as they so often do, so I decided to let them dictate the way this book would take shape. I took it home, lovingly covered each page with appropriate pet-related paper, and added photos and anecdotes of my darling companions.

Materials
❋ child's board book (about 5" × 6" [13cm × 15cm])
❋ sanding sponge
❋ patterned paper (1 sheet for the cover and 1 for each inside page spread)
❋ adhesive
❋ brayer
❋ scissors

Actual size: 5" × 6" (13cm × 15cm)

Supplies: Cardstock; patterned paper (Around the Block, SEI); rub-ons, stickers (Adornit, American Crafts, Arctic Frog, Doodlebug, SEI); brads, clips (Creative Impressions); stapler (Close to My Heart); stamps (Close to My Heart, Hot Off the Press, My Sentiments Exactly, Purple Onion); ribbon (Adornit, Creative Imaginations, Creative Impressions); frames, tabs, tags (SEI); ink (Clearsnap, Tsukineko); acrylic paint (Ranger); pens (American Crafts, Uni-ball); adhesive (Beacon)

1. Peel off glossy layer
Peel off the glossy layer of the book's cover to reveal the bare chipboard.

2. Sand edges of cover
Sand the edges with a sanding sponge until smooth.

3. Cover chipboard covers
Lay your patterned paper face down. Add adhesive to the front cover of the board book and set the book, cover side down, along the left edge of the paper. Add adhesive to the spine and the back cover of the book and fold over the paper to cover it completely. Use a brayer to smooth out the paper.

4. Trim paper
Trim the paper so it fits the book. Then repeat all the steps for the inside pages. For step 3, open up the inside pages and apply adhesive, then set them face down onto the patterned paper to attach.

Look for Playful Elements

To add a twist to your mini album, look for board books with interactive elements. I chose a book with pull tabs, which I used to hide journaling.

Coffee Cup Album

I admit it. I'm a huge fan of Starbucks lattes. In fact, it was after ordering one that I got some grande inspiration along with my change. I thought the gorgeously illustrated holiday cup would make a great cover for an album about what makes me happy. Filling the book came easily, but finding a way to keep the album shut eluded me. I tried the conventional ways like using ribbon. Nothing worked. In desperation, I grabbed a coffee cup sleeve … and voila! I got the perfect closure for a coffee-inspired album.

Actual size: 5" × 5" (13cm × 13cm)

Supplies: Cardstock (Bazzill, WorldWin); patterned paper (Fancy Pants, Scenic Route); letter stickers (American Crafts); cardstock button (Prima); ribbon (Creative Impressions); inks (Clearsnap, Tsukineko); pens (Sakura, Sanford) paint pen (Marvy)

Materials
- 16 oz. paper coffee cup
- scissors
- chalk ink (optional)
- pen
- patterned paper (4 sheets, double-sided heavyweight)
- adhesive
- bone folder
- paper piercer
- large needle
- embroidery floss
- coffee cup sleeve

86

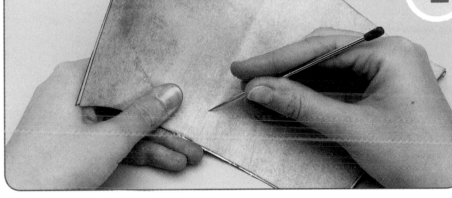

1. Cut bottom off coffee cup

Cut down the seam of the coffee cup, then cut in a circle to remove the bottom of the cup. Gently flatten the cup. (It's OK if you create creases along the lip of the cup.) Trim all edges of the cup (except the lip at the top) so they are smooth. Ink the edges if desired. This will be your album's cover.

2. Trace coffee cup and cut out pages

Open the flattened cup and trace it four times onto the patterned paper (one on each page). Cut out the patterned paper shapes.

3. Fold pages in half

Adhere one piece of paper to the inside of the flattened coffee cup (the inside of the front and back covers). Then fold the other three paper pages in half. Be careful to line up all the edges evenly. Set the crease with a bone folder. Ink the edges of the pages, if desired.

4. Poke holes for binding

Open the coffee cup cover and stack the opened paper pages inside. Using the paper piercer, poke two holes along the fold line through all the pages and the cover, about ¾" (2cm) from the bottom and ¾" (2cm) from the top.

5. Thread floss for binding

Thread embroidery floss through the needle. Then stitch through the two holes in the spine to bind your album. Start on the inside and thread the needle through the top hole to the outside, leaving about 2" (5cm) of thread hanging on the inside. Then thread the needle through the bottom hole from outside to inside.

6. Tie floss to secure

Tie the two ends of thread in a knot. Your knot should be on the inside of the album in the fold.

7. Embellish album and sleeve

Embellish your coffee cup album. Add your title to the coffee cup sleeve. Insert your album into the sleeve. If the sleeve doesn't sit high enough, open the seam of the sleeve and re-attach it so the opening is larger.

Cover Up

You might want to cover up any logos or writing on your coffee cup sleeve so the album title stands out. Punch cardstock with a large circle punch and attach it right over the logo before adding your title.

Tabs in the Round

I love using ribbon and fabric to create tabs and dividers for my albums, but sometimes I need to mix it up a bit! Creating simple, graphic-looking tags is easy. Simply cut circles with a 1" (3cm) circle punch and attach half the circle to a page.

Displaying & Storing Mini Albums

Displaying mini albums makes so much more sense to me than showing off larger ones. Guests are much more likely to flip through a mini album than to take out a huge book. I tend to rotate albums in a few designated spots around the living room, but you can show off your work anywhere you want!

※ Store your mini albums in a basket beside the couch. This way people can browse through them while they lounge.

※ Set up a display of several mini albums on a small wall shelf. Keep them at a height that's easy to reach so people can easily view them.

※ Take a couple of your mini books to work and display them on your desk. I guarantee your coworkers won't be able to resist taking a peek! (You may even get requests to make a few.)

※ Line up your mini albums along a mantle or windowsill. Keep in mind that if you have a lot of sunlight coming through your windows, you'll want to move your albums every so often so the paper doesn't become bleached from the sun.

※ Store albums that aren't on display in a fire-safe, plastic bin. Put albums in photo-safe page protectors. And avoid piling tons of weighty albums on top of each other, in order to protect the albums at the bottom.

Painted Paper Bag Album

Paper bags don't need to be limited to food-related albums like my recipe book (on page 72). There are so many things to do with them, the possibilities are endless! For this one, I wanted to make a rustic-looking, Halloween-themed album. I started by painting paper bags in Halloween colors, then added lots of rough and worn details like torn paper, inking and frayed ribbon. I think my album is both rustic and "boo-tiful." Don't you?

Actual size: 5½" × 5½" (14cm × 14cm)

Supplies: Cardstock; patterned paper (American Traditional, BoBunny, Die Cuts With A View, Doodlebug, Making Memories, Moxxie, Rusty Pickle, Scenic Route); ribbon (Creative Imaginations, Daisy D's); twine (Creative Impressions); stickers (Daisy D's, Reminisce, Rusty Pickle); buttons, chipboard letters, die-cut shapes (Daisy D's); labels (Around the Block, Dymo); trim (Doodlebug); paint (DecoArt, Plaid); ink (Tsukineko); pen (American Crafts)

Materials

Album
- paper lunch bags (4)
- newspaper or paper towel
- acrylic paint, various colors
- paintbrush
- heat gun (optional)
- paper trimmer or scissors
- ribbon (2 pieces, 8" [20cm] each)
- adhesive
- patterned paper (3 sheets)
- decorative-edge scissors
- Crop-A-Dile
- ribbon pieces (at least 6)

Fraying Ribbon
- heavily woven ribbon (at least ½" [1cm] wide)
- scissors

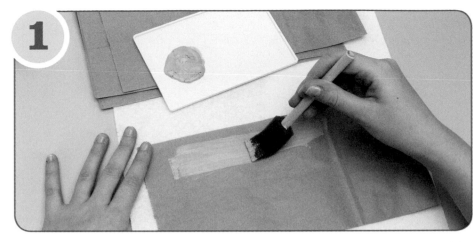

1. Paint paper bags
Lay a paper bag on newspaper or a paper towel. Brush on various colors of paint; it's OK if paints mix and the brush strokes are uneven. Paint until the whole bag is covered and let the paint dry before painting the other side of the bag. (You can use a heat gun to speed up the drying process.) Paint the remaining bags and let them dry as well.

2. Cut ends off bags
Trim about ¼" (6mm) off the edges of the closed ends of the bags.

3. Stack and fold bags
Stack the paper bags horizontally with the bottom flaps up, and alternate the ends (i.e., one bag with the bottom to the left, the next bag with the bottom to the right, etc.). Fold the stack in half to create a book with square pages.

4. Add ribbon to covers
Attach one piece of ribbon horizontally to the middle of the front cover of the book. The ribbon should be placed about halfway into the cover, with about 5" (13cm) hanging off the edge of the album. Turn the album over and attach the other piece of ribbon to the back cover in the same way.

5. Cut paper and attach to bags
Cut 12 pieces of patterned paper to 5" × 5" (13cm × 13cm). Tear some of the edges of the paper squares. With the adhesive, attach a square to each page in the album as well as to the front and back covers (over the ribbon).

6. Cut paper and attach to spine
Cut a piece of patterned paper to 1¾" × 5" (4cm × 13cm). Trim the two long sides using the decorative-edge scissors. Then fold the paper in half lengthwise. Attach the paper to the spine of the album, half on the front cover and half on the back.

7. Punch holes in album
Punch six holes, about 1" (3cm) apart, down the left side of the album.

8. Tie ribbon through holes
Tie ribbons through the holes and double knot them.

▶ Fray Ribbon
Ribbon that is heavily woven frays easily. To fray, simply cut a piece of ribbon in half lengthwise, and pull at the threads until they come loose.

On the Fray
Frayed ribbon adds a rough feel perfect for painted paper bag albums.

ADMIT ONE 4
SPOOKY
FUN

Ready Yeti?

HAPPY

HAUNTING

CAn d

Peanut/Arachide
m

Cadbury
mini

SWEET TREATS

HOCUS POCUS

Framed!

Painting photo edges is a simple and unique way to create a photo frame. Using a bright color is also a great way to distinguish the edges of a dark photo against a black cardstock background. Since you already have your paint out, why not give it a try? To add a bit of color, simply dip a sponge brush or makeup sponge into a small amount of paint. Drag the brush in small strokes along the edges of the photo.

Mix-It-Up Album

Once you've crafted a bunch of innovative albums, take advantage of your leftovers and create a one-of-a-kind mix-it-up book—basically a jumble of leftover elements like bits of cardboard, chipboard pages, coffee cup sleeves and all sorts of other stuff. The beauty of making an album like this is that there are no rules—anything goes!—and the fun of it is seeing what kind of outrageous things you can add.

Actual size: 6" × 6" (15cm × 15cm)

Supplies: Mini album pages (BasicGrey, BoBunny, Maya Road); cardstock; patterned paper (Die Cuts With A View, Making Memories, Scenic Route); chipboard accents (Maya Road, Scenic Route); stickers (Adornit, American Crafts); Junkitz, Making Memories, Paper Studio, Scenic Route); ribbon (Bazzill, other); cards (7gypsics); buttons (Making Memories, other); tag (American Crafts); fabric tape (Imagination Project); twine (Creative Impressions); labels (Dymo); 24/7 cards (My Mind's Eye); paint (Ranger); inks (Clearsnap, Marvy, Sakura)

Materials

Album
* leftovers (album pages, transparency scraps, playing cards, coasters, corrugated cardboard, etc.)
* hole punch or Crop-A-Dile
* pen or pencil
* binder rings or ribbon

Transparency Technique
* acrylic paint (1 light color)

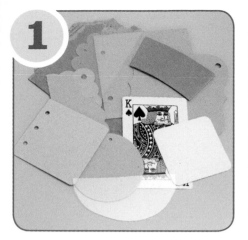

1. Gather and arrange materials
Gather an assortment of materials to include in your album—leftover album pages, transparency scraps, playing cards, coasters, corrugated cardboard, etc. Place the largest pieces in front and back to use as your covers. Arrange the rest of the pages so that you get an even distribution of sizes and materials. In other words, don't put two of the same type of pages (like two transparencies or two playing cards) next to each other. Embellish the pages as desired.

2. Punch holes and bind album
If the covers don't already have holes, punch holes. Then stack the materials so they are somewhat aligned on the left side. Use the holes in the cover to mark holes for the inside pages. (Some of your pages may already have holes in them. If so, you can adjust the placement of the pages to align with other pages' holes, or just punch new holes. This is a mix-it-up album, so feel free to mix it up as you want!) Punch holes in the pages, and insert binder rings or ribbons to bind.

3. Make a transparency pocket
Try this technique for creating the perfect mix-it-up style journaling spot for tranparencies or acrylic pages. Use your finger to paint on white or light-colored acrylic paint. Let the paint dry and write away!

Clearly Fabulous
It's clear: Transparencies make great pockets and pages. But a piece of transparency also adds an interesting layer of dimension to covers. To re-create the look of my dimensional Mix-It-Up cover, first decorate your cover with paper and chipboard shapes. Then cut a piece of transparency to the width of the cover. Add some dimensional alphas to the transparency and then bind the cover and transparency.

4

chapter

think outside
THE BOX

Crafting Unique Mini Album Gifts

Birthdays, holidays, baby showers, Mother's Day: The gift-giving season is endless! Fortunately for me, I love giving gifts. But there are always people who are hard to buy for—either they're "particular" or they just seem to have everything. Whatever the case, making a gift is the way to go. Giving a unique gift from the heart is something the recipient is guaranteed not to have already, and guaranteed to love! In this chapter you will find unique project ideas that make fabulous gifts … even if only for yourself.

Tag Album and Gift Box

Welcome to the Neighbor

the best Sushi
Ladner Sushi
Located in Ladner Village
on 48th Ave.

Materials

Album
* Small Tag Template (page 124)
* cardstock (1 sheet)
* pen
* scissors
* patterned paper (1 sheet, heavyweight)
* hole punch or Crop-A-Dile
* large eyelets (6)
* eyelet setter and craft hammer or Crop-A-Dile
* binder ring or ribbon

Box
* take-out box (clean)
* patterned paper
* embellishments
* ribbon

When we moved to Vancouver, we didn't know anyone or where anything was. Where is the nearest craft store? Dog park? Library? What is the best pizza place? Hair salon? Restaurant? I greatly appreciated neighborly advice for places worth visiting (and avoiding). Now I return the favor, but in my own scrappy way, of course. I write community details on cardstock tags and deliver them to new neighbors in an adorable take-out container. Just like a good neighbor, scrapbookers are there.

Actual size (of album): 2½ × 3½ (9cm × 6cm)

Supplies: Cardstock; patterned paper (SEI); ribbon, rickrack (American Crafts, Creative Impressions, Daisy D's); eyelets (Provo Craft); ink (Clearsnap); pen (Sakura); Misc: buttons, fabric strips

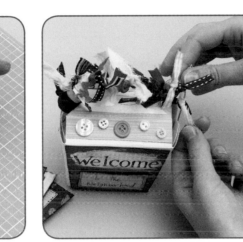

1. Cut out patterned paper
Trace the Small Tag Template (on page 124) onto cardstock six times. Cut out each tag. Trace the tag template onto patterned paper six times and cut out the tags. Attach each paper tag to a cardstock tag.

2. Punch holes in tags
Punch a hole in the narrow end of one of the tags. Use this hole as a guide to punch holes in the other tags. Then embellish your pages.

3. Set eyelets
Insert a large eyelet into each hole and set with an eyelet setter and craft hammer (or use a Crop-A-Dile). Insert a binder ring or ribbon to bind your pages. Stick your album inside the take-out box and deliver!

Embellish the box
Cut out patterned paper to fit over the front and back of the box and on top. Add the "Welcome to the Neighborhood" greeting, and attach buttons or other embellishments to the top. Finish by tying ribbon scraps to the handle of the box.

Photo Blocks

Photo blocks are a go-to gift! Depending on the photos, you can make them for any occasion: a new baby, Christmas, birthday, graduation, family reunion, wedding and more. They are fun and easy to make and perfect for displaying on a shelf, a desk or the coffee table. Plus, they make an excellent conversation piece! Try making them in various sizes. Any wooden blocks will work as long as they are perfectly proportioned on each side. Add doodles, stickers or rub-ons, or even have your kids create some artwork to be featured on the blocks.

Materials
* 3-4 wooden blocks (2" [5cm] cubes)
* sanding sponge
* paper trimmer or scissors
* patterned paper (1 sheet)
* adhesive
* brayer
* paintbrush
* decoupage medium

Actual size: 2" × 2" × 2" (5cm × 5cm × 5cm)

Supplies: Patterned paper (BasicGrey, Karen Foster, KI Memories, Rhonna Designs); rub-ons (Adornit); sticker (SEI); pen (American Crafts)

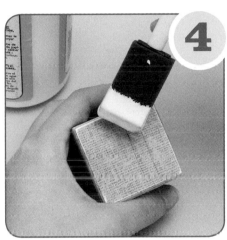

1. Sand blocks
Using the sanding sponge, rigorously sand each block until the sides are smooth and the corners are slightly rounded.

2. Cut squares and attach
Cut photos and patterned paper into 1⅞" (5cm) squares. Attach one square to each side of each block. Smooth out any air bubbles with the brayer.

3. Sand edges
Quickly sand the edges and corners of each block to give them a slightly distressed and smooth look. Be careful not to scratch your photos (other than on the edges).

4. Apply decoupage medium
Add any flat embellishments like rub-ons or stickers. Brush decoupage medium over the entire block, making sure to cover everything. Brush out any glops of decoupage medium. Allow the blocks to dry.

Be My Valentine
Photo blocks make greats gifts for any occasion! Make a love-themed set like this one for Valentine's Day. Or make one for your parents' anniversary. Make others to celebrate a sister's birthday or to welcome a new baby.

Spiral-Bound Chipboard Album

As an alternative to giving new parents a regular baby card, how about creating a small "welcome baby" mini album instead? It will most definitely be treasured and be a memento to keep forever. The arrival of my youngest niece, Hannah, prompted me to put together a mini book to fit this very special occasion. Like its name suggests, this wee book is full of charming quotes focused on the littlest member of our family.

Actual size: 6" × 3½" (15cm × 9cm)

Supplies: Cardstock; patterned paper (Doodlebug, KI Memories, Making Memories); chipboard letters (BasicGrey); jell accent, stickers (Doodlebug); rub-ons (Doodlebug, Junkitz); metal plaque (Making Memories); ribbon (Creative Impressions); ink (Clearsnap, Tsukineko); paint (Ranger); quotes (We Scrap); Misc: pacifier, transparency

Materials
* patterned paper and/or cardstock (2 sheets)
* paper trimmer or scissors
* sewing machine (or needle) and thread
* thin chipboard (1 sheet)
* adhesive
* brayer
* Bind-it-All machine
* Bind-it-All coil (⅝")

1. Cut paper and stitch borders
Cut 10 pieces of paper that measure 6" × 3½" (15cm × 9cm). Using a sewing machine (or needle and thread for hand stitching) stitch a border around each piece of paper.

2. Cut out chipboard pieces
Cut five pieces of chipboard that measure 6" × 3½" (15cm × 9cm).

3. Attach paper to pages
Attach the stitched papers to both sides of the chipboard pages. Smooth out any air bubbles with the brayer.

4. Bind pages
Using the Bind-it-All machine, punch the binding holes along the left edge of each page. Insert the coils in the Bind-it-All with the album and bind the pages together. Alternatively, you can bind the album with binder rings.

Paint on Texture

I love the textured look that paint adds to album pages, but printing over lumpy paint is not the best idea. To get the look without the lump, simply print words onto a transparency and cut them out. Then paint the back side of the transparency (behind the letters) with white paint.

Textured Lid

the Learning OF snow balls

Kids of all ages love snow. When I studied the tin protecting an accordion-fold album, the kid in me imagined it as a snowball. The challenge was making a flat tin lid resemble snow. A trip to Grouse Mountain with Brent, my friend Jodi and her daughter Dasha, provided me with snow photos, a mini album theme and a snow-making brainwave. A combination of gesso, dimensional paint and sparkles became my snowball. Try it the next time you need a unique gift box. It's "snow" much fun!

Actual size: 5" (13cm) in diameter

Supplies: Album and tin (EK Success); patterned paper (BasicGrey, Scenic Route); rub-ons, stickers (American Crafts, Arctic Frog, BasicGrey, Reminisce); labels (Around the Block, Dymo); texture paint (Delta); ribbon, rickrack (American Crafts, Creative Impressions); rhinestones (Heidi Swapp); ink (Tsukineko); pens (Sakura, Sanford)

Materials
tin lid
paintbrush
gesso
palette knife
dimensional paint, white
    (like Texture Magic)
glitter (white)
letter stickers

1. Brush lid with gesso and paint
Paint the top of the lid with a thick layer of gesso. The more uneven the better! Let it dry. Then, using a palette knife, spread a thick layer of dimensional paint over the top of the tin. Let that dry.

2. Add more gesso and paint
Add another layer of gesso using the palette knife, but don't let it dry. Right away, add another thick layer of dimensional paint, creating peaks. Move on to the next steps quickly before the paint dries.

3. Sprinkle lid with glitter
While the paint is still wet, sprinkle glitter lightly over the entire lid.

4. Add embellishments
Also while the paint is wet, embed letter stickers gently into the dimensional paint. You can also embed other stickers and thin metal or chipboard. Allow the paint to dry.

(Not the) Letter of the Law

There's no rule that says you have to stick to one kind of letter or number in an album. Play with various alphas on the same project: mix up sizes, fonts, textures and colors to add a playful, funky look to your book.

Fabric Album

I am not a seamstress, but my mother is a fabulous one. I do share Mum's love of fabric, and I enjoy incorporating fabric bits into my scrapbooks. I've always wanted to make a paperless mini album. During a delightful search through Mum's fabric scraps I felt inspired to make a fabric album tribute, of course! This one is dedicated to my mum.

Actual size: 5" × 6" (13cm × 15cm)

Supplies: Fabric; fabric glue and stiffener (Beacon); canvas paper (Hahnemuhle); adhesive linen (Close to My Heart); buttons (Creative Imaginations, Making Memories); ribbon, rickrack (Creative Impressions); Misc: eyelets, felt, floss, thread

Materials

Album
- ❂ linen (1 yard)
- ❂ fabric pieces (12)
- ❂ rotary cutter
- ❂ ruler
- ❂ cutting mat
- ❂ sewing machine and thread
- ❂ fabric glue (optional)
- ❂ Crop-A-Dile
- ❂ grommets (6)
- ❂ grommet setter
- ❂ hammer
- ❂ binder ring

Fabric Embellishments
- ❂ fabric pieces
- ❂ plastic
- ❂ fabric stiffener
- ❂ paintbrush
- ❂ punches and/or scissors

1. Cut fabric
Using the rotary cutter and ruler (and cutting mat to protect your work surface) cut 12 pieces of linen to 5" × 6" (13cm × 15cm). Cut 12 pieces of other fabric to about 3¾" × 4¾" (10cm × 12cm).

2. Stitch fabric together
Sew a fabric piece to the front of each linen piece. Stitch on photos and embellishments. You can attach them with fabric glue to keep them in place while sewing.

3. Sew pages together
Stack two linen pieces with the wrong (empty) sides together. Stitch the pieces together around all the edges.

4. Insert grommets
Punch a hole in the upper left corner of each page. Insert grommets into the holes. Using a grommet-setting tool and a hammer, set each grommet. Insert a binder ring to bind the pages.

Add Easy Fabric Embellishments
Lay a piece of fabric over plastic (like a page protector) and apply fabric stiffener with a brush. Let it dry for several hours. Use a punch to cut out shapes.

"Canvas" Your Album
To keep your book totally textile, use printable canvas to make photos and journaling strips for your pages. Just print like you would onto regular printer paper.

CD Case Album

My best friend has been in my life since we were five years old. To show Britt just what our special relationship means to me, I made this mini book focused on us, using a clear CD jewel case. Thinking thin, I chose to use an accordion-pleated format that would fit neatly into the case, allowing it to close easily. It can be tucked into a purse, or displayed open on a shelf or tabletop. This is a quick and easy gift but a thoughtful way to say "thanks, friend."

Actual size: 5½" × 4¾" (14cm × 12cm)

Supplies: Patterned paper (BasicGrey, Fancy Pants, Scenic Route); rub-ons, stickers (American Crafts, Scenic Route); chipboard brackets (Heidi Swapp); ink (Clearsnap); pen (Sakura)

Materials
* patterned paper (2 sheets, double-sided, heavyweight)
* paper trimmer with scoring blade
* adhesive
* CD jewel case

108

1. Cut and score paper
Cut two strips of patterned paper to 12" × 4⅝" (30cm × 12cm). Score each strip at 4¾" (12cm) and 9½" (24cm) from the left edge. (See How to Score with a Trimmer on page 9 if needed.)

2. Attach paper strips
Attach the left end of one strip to the top of the right end of another. The smallest section (2½" [6cm] wide) should be attached to the bottom of the 4¾" (12cm) section on the other strip.

3. Attach paper to CD case
Cut two pieces of patterned paper, one measuring 4⅝" × 4¾" (12cm × 12cm) and the other 5½" × 4⅝" (14cm × 12cm). Set the smaller piece aside. Attach the larger piece to the inside back cover of the CD case.

4. Attach pages to CD case
Adhere the smallest (2½" [6cm]) section of the long cardstock strip to the inside back cover of the jewel case (over the paper you attached in step 3). Attach the strip to the left half of the CD case.

5. Complete album
Attach the remaining paper square from step 3 to the inside back cover, over the top of the small section on the strip of cardstock. Fold the strip accordion-style (with mountain and valley folds) to fit in the jewel case.

Felt Play Book

This soft idea came to me when I rediscovered the fabric touch book my mother sewed for me when I was young. I loved feeling the different fabrics and interacting with the scenes she created. Though my first love is paper, I enjoy experimenting with other mediums, and a book for a kid just called for felt. Plus, felt is easy to work with. Hannah's felt book is small, cute and easy to carry, just like she is!

Actual size: 5½" × 7" (14cm × 18cm)

Supplies: Felt; buttons, flowers (Creative Imaginations); large felt letter (Jo-Ann's); paint pen (Marvy); fabric paint (Pebeo); adhesive (Beacon); Misc: fabric, transparency, Velcro

Materials

* felt (at least 8 sheets: 2 white, 2 black, 2 light blue, 1 purple and various other colors as desired)
* rotary cutter
* ruler
* cutting mat
* paper trimmer or scissors
* transparencies (3 sheets)
* sewing machine and thread
* fabric glue
* Velcro, rough side (about 9" [23cm])
* embroidery needle
* floss

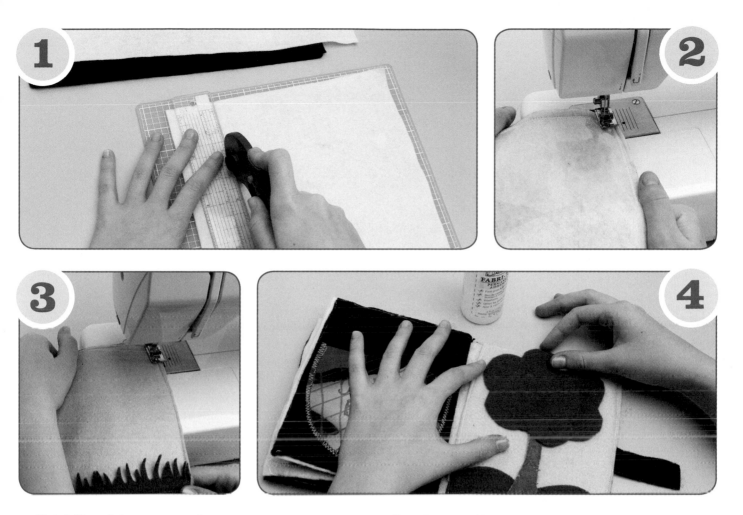

1. Cut felt and transparencies

Using the rotary cutter and ruler (and cutting mat to protect your work surface), cut four pieces of felt to 7" × 11" (18cm × 28cm) (two white and two black). Then cut the two blue pieces of felt to 5½" × 6¾" (14cm × 17cm). Next, cut one piece of purple felt to 2" × 6¾" (5cm × 17cm). (Add a wavy border to the long edges if you like). Using the paper trimmer, cut three pieces of transparencies to about 5" × 4" (13cm × 10cm). You can cut one in a basket shape and another with a wavy edge, if you like.

2. Sew on transparency pockets and spine

Orient your pieces of felt so the long sides are at the top. Sew each transparency like a pocket (just on three sides) onto the left half of three pieces of felt (two white pieces and one black). On the remaining black piece, sew the purple felt strip to the center (with the short sides of the purple piece at the top and bottom). Now, stack your felt pieces as follows: the black piece with the purple strip face down; a white piece with a transparency face up; the black piece with a transparency face down; a white piece with a transparency face up.

3. Sew felt together

Sew the bottom two pieces of felt together in a border all the way around. Then place a blue piece of felt over the top (white) right side of the stack. Stitch the blue piece on. Next, sew the remaining two pieces of felt together and add a blue piece in the same way. Stack the two completed rectangles and fold them in half—this is your book. The purple strip should be attached to the spine of the book, and each inside page spread should have a transparency.

4. Cut out and glue felt shapes

Cut out various shapes from the other colors of felt to glue to the three inside right-hand pages: tree tops and trunks, grass and hills, a basket with flower stems, etc. Using fabric glue, adhere these to the pages.

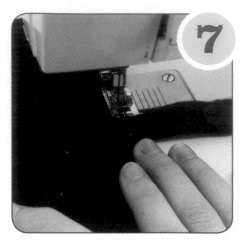

5. Glue Velcro to felt shapes

Cut additional shapes out of felt to finish off the "pictures" on your pages: a sun, trees, birds, flowers, fruit, etc. Cut a small piece of Velcro (the rough side) for each shape and glue the Velcro onto the backs of the shapes using fabric glue. Put some of the shapes in the pockets and Velcro some to the pages.

6. Hand stitch binding

Thread your needle with several strands (6–8) of embroidery floss. Open up your album and turn it so the cover is face up. Stitch down the center of the purple spine to bind the pages using whatever you like.

7. Sew on tab closure

Finally, create your tab closure. Cut a piece of black felt to 3" × 1" (8cm × 3cm). Glue a small piece of Velcro to one end. Then sew about ½" (1cm) of the strip (Velcro face down) to the outside of the back cover. Velcro the tab to the front cover to close.

Accessorize!

When stitching felt, remember that this mini book is for a child. Using uneven stitches will add a whimsical, childlike quality to the book. Pre-made, felt embellishments are the perfect accessories for your book.

Child's Play

This is the perfect mini book to involve children in the making of. Engage them in the creation! Let a child draw a picture and use that as the base for your felt pages. Have a child attach self-adhesive Velcro to the felt shapes. Allow a child to draw on the transparencies with a paint pen and then fill up pockets with felt shapes. They will love sharing "their" book, which will likely become a treasure of childhood.

Mini Album Gifts

The best thing about mini albums is that they make great gifts for everyone!
You can give a mini book as a gift for any occasion or even "just because."
Here are some ideas for great gift inspirations:

❀ Give a fabric book to a mom who quilts for Mother's Day.
❀ Give a clear badge "brag book" to new parents. Just embellish the outside of the pockets and let them insert their own photos as baby grows.
❀ Give an "I'm Thinking About You" laminated pouch album for anyone who is miles away—the small, thin size is easy to mail.
❀ Give a jewel case album with wedding photos to newlyweds, and include a CD with additional photos or a compilation of music from their wedding.
❀ Make a desktop flip book filled with kids' photos for Father's Day.
❀ Give a teacher "thank you" photo blocks with photos from the school year.
❀ Make an inspirational coin envelope book for someone who needs a little lift.

Desktop Flip Album

I am always amazed at the energy my parents muster whenever my nieces come to visit. They seem filled with new life, renewed vigor and delight in each and every moment spent together. My nieces also blossom in the presence of their grandparents. When they are together, life is truly grand. To capture this mutual *joie de vivre* I designed a stand-alone, desk-style flip book. Of course, my mother flipped over it.

Materials
❋ chipboard (1 sheet)
❋ cardstock (1 sheet)
❋ paper trimmer with scoring blade
❋ adhesive
❋ Crop-A-Dile
❋ ribbon (2 pieces, 5" [13cm] each)
❋ patterned paper (3 sheets, double-sided, heavy weight)
❋ binder rings (2)

Actual size: 5" × 5" (13cm × 13cm)

Supplies: Cardstock; patterned paper (Deja Views, KI Memories); chipboard and rub-on letters, photo corner (American Crafts); rhinestones (Doodlebug, Gel-a-Tins, Prima); clips (Making Memories); glitter dimensional paint (Ranger); ribbon (Creative Impressions, May Arts); inks (Close to My Heart, Clearsnap, Tsukineko)

1. Cut chipboard and cardstock

Cut a piece of chipboard to 10" × 5" (25cm × 13cm). Attach the scoring blade to your trimmer. Set a strip of cardstock horizontally in the trimmer. Score the strip down the center. Replace the scoring blade in your trimmer with the cutting blade. Cut a piece of cardstock to 10" × 5" (25cm × 13cm). Adhere it to the chipboard.

2. Cover chipboard with cardstock and punch holes

Fold the strip in half at the score line (and keep it folded for the remaining steps). Next, punch two holes through both sides of the chipboard about 3" (8cm) apart along the edge opposite the fold.

3. Finish punching holes

Now punch two holes about 2" (5cm) apart along the folded side of the chipboard.

4. Tie on ribbon

Pull one piece of ribbon through a hole on the open (not folded) side of the chipboard. Insert it into the hole on the opposite side. Tie a knot in the ribbon on the outsides of the chipboard. Repeat with the other ribbon and holes.

5. Cut and add pages

Cut nine pieces of patterned paper to 4½" × 4½" (11cm × 11cm). Embellish as desired. Using the holes 2" (5cm) apart on the chipboard as a guide, punch holes at the top of each page. Insert binder rings through the holes at the top, and add the pages.

Double Take

If you have a lot of photos to include, take advantage of both sides of each page. Just flip the album to display photos on the backside. It'll be double the pictures and double the fun!

Grandmas are earth angels

Coin Envelope Album

With so many spots to tuck tiny treasures, coin envelope albums make great little mini book gifts! These small paper envelopes dressed in feminine details turned out to be an ideal format for sharing favorite inspirational quotes and sayings when someone needs a little pick me up—a great gift for any of my female friends. Deciding exactly which quotes to use was the hardest thing to do when making this pretty little album.

Actual size: 2½" x 4" (6cm x 10cm)

Supplies: Patterned paper, ribbon, tags (My Little Shoebox); ink (Clearsnap); adhesive (Therm O Web); Misc: clip, fabric, foam tape, making tape

Materials
* 15 coin envelopes (2½" × 4"[(6cm × 10cm])
* scissors
* paper trimmer
* patterned paper (2 sheets)
* circle punch (¾" [2cm])
* double-sided tape or tape runner
* chipboard (1 sheet)
* masking tape
* pen
* liquid glue (like Zip Dry)
* magnet closure
* sanding sponge (optional)
* chalk ink (optional)
* tags (15)

1. Cut off ends and punch circles

Trim all the flaps off the coin envelopes. Then punch a half circle at the top of each envelope.

2. Cut and attach paper

Cut 30 pieces of patterned paper to 4¼" × 1½" (11cm × 4cm). Fold each piece in half lengthwise. Wrap a folded piece around the edge of an envelope (one-half of the strip on each side) and adhere as shown. Adhere a strip to the other side of the envelope. Repeat for the other envelopes.

3. Tape and stack envelopes

Add double-sided tape (or use a tape runner) down the middle of both sides of 13 envelopes. Apply tape to only one side of the remaining two envelopes. Stack the envelopes; the two with only one taped side should be at the top and bottom of the stack with the un-taped sides facing out. Now all the envelopes shuld be attached to one another.

4. Cut chipboard and tape

Cut five pieces of chipboard as follows: two pieces to 4½" × 2¾" (11cm × 7cm); 2 pieces to 2¾" × 1" (7cm × 3cm), and 1 piece to 2¾" × 2¾" (7cm × 7cm). Snip the top two corners off the last piece. Cut five pieces of patterned paper to the same dimensions. Then, lay out the chipboard pieces in this order: the tag-shaped piece, a 1" (3cm) piece, a 4½" (11cm) piece, a 1" (3cm) piece, and a 4½" (11cm) piece. Using masking tape, tape the ends together (as shown) so that you have one long strip of cardstock.

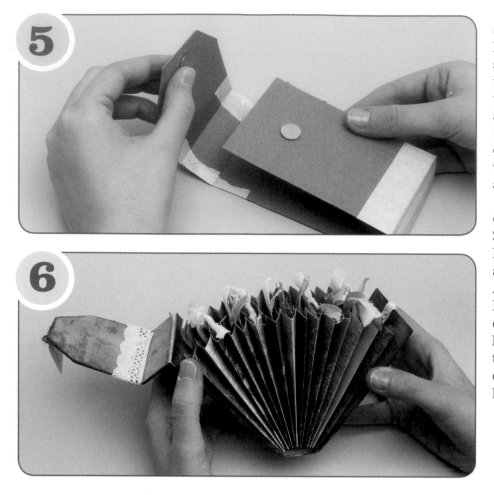

5. Add magnet closure

Fold the chipboard so you can see how it will close. Mark where the magnet closure will go: on the underside of the flap (inside the album) and on top of the front, 4½" (11cm) piece. Glue on the magnet closures. Cover the entire album cover with the patterned paper pieces. Sand and ink the edges, if desired.

6. Attach envelopes to cover

Slide the tags inside the envelopes. Next, apply glue to the two envelopes at the front and back of the stack. Add glue to the bottom of the stack. Insert the stack into the chipboard cover, attaching the two sides and bottom of the stack of envelopes to the cover. Gently check that everything opens easily, then allow the liquid glue to dry.

Clip It, Clip It Good

With their many colors, bulldog clips make great additions to any mini album. Use them as dividers to highlight certain pages, or use them just to dress up an album. Here, I used a pretty bulldog clip to hold my title, a tiny tag hanging in the jaws of the clip.

Tag, You're It!

You can include a variety of tags in your envelope album.
Gather pre-cut tags you already have and add photos and quotes,
or cut your own from heavyweight patterned paper. Whatever
you choose, add loops of ribbon to the tops for easy removal and
make sure the tags are smaller than 4" × 2¼" (10cm × 6cm) so
they'll fit inside the album.

Exploding Box Album

I've been told that this little box gives repeated delight to anyone receiving it. I have made and given away several, and I always get an "explosive" reaction. Making one for the first time may seem a little daunting, but if you persevere you will be delighted with the end result. You'll soon find yourself making one for all your loved ones. This is one of those projects that begs to be made again and again once you understand the assembling process. This time, it's okay to think inside the box!

Materials

* cardstock (3 sheets:
  12" × 12" [30cm × 30cm],
  11" × 11" [28cm × 28cm],
  10½" × 10½" [27cm × 27cm])
* patterned paper (1 sheet, heavy-weight, 8" × 8" [20cm × 20cm])
* paper trimmer with scoring blade
* scissors
* circle punch (no bigger than 1" [3cm]
* adhesive
* paper-clip (optional)

Actual size (closed): 4" × 4" (10cm × 10cm)

Supplies: Cardstock (Bazzill, WorldWin); overlays, patterned paper (Tada Creative); brad, clip, ribbons (Creative Impressions); mesh (Magic Mesh); jewels (Doodlebug); transparent tree (Making Memories); rub-ons (Daisy D's); flocking (Stampendous); ink (All My Memories, Clearsnap, Tsukineko); paint (Ranger); water colors (Sakura); pens (Sakura, Zebra); adhesive (Beacon, Glue Dots, Sakura, Xyron)

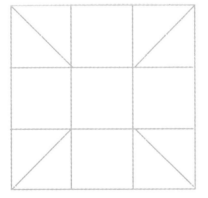

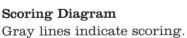

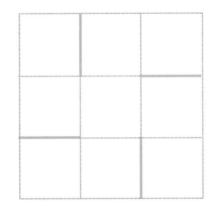

Scoring Diagram
Gray lines indicate scoring.

Cutting Diagram
Green lines indicate cutting.

1. Score cardstock

Score the 12" (30cm) sheet of cardstock at 4" (10cm) from the left edge. (See How to Score with a Trimmer on page 9 if needed.) Turn the sheet 90 degrees and score at 4" (10cm) again. Turn the page another 90 degrees and score at 4" (10cm), and then a final 90 degrees and score at 4" (10cm). You should now have a sheet with nine squares. Score a diagonal line (toward the center) on the four corner squares. (See scoring diagram). You may need to fold your sheet to fit it in the trimmer.

2. Score and cut second sheet

Repeat step 1 with the 11" (28cm) sheet of cardstock; this time score at 3¾" (10cm) instead of 4" (10cm). Then cut the top edge of the bottom, left square. Turn your page 90 degrees and repeat. Then repeat for the other two sides. (See cutting diagram.) Fold each of the four corner squares over the square to its right. Trim off any excess that hangs over. You should now have a cross shape.

3. Punch half-circles

Orient your cross shape so the squares that fold over are on top. On the square at the top of the cross, punch a half-circle in the top edge of the square that is folded over. Rotate the cross 90 degrees three times to punch half-circles at the tops of the other three folded-over squares. These are the beginnings of the pockets on the inside of your box.

4. Finish pockets

At the top of the cross shape, on the square underneath (without the half-circle), add a thin line of adhesive to the bottom and right sides. Press the top square (with the half-circle) down to adhere it to the other square. You should now have a pocket. Repeat three more times to create pockets out of the other three square sections. You should now have four pockets.

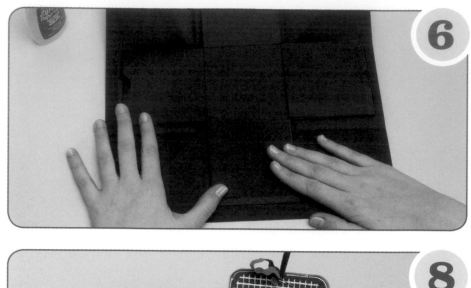

5. Attach cardstock sheets

Add adhesive to the center square on your first (12" [30cm]) sheet of cardstock. Adhere the center square of your second sheet (the cross shape) to the first sheet. Make sure the pockets are facing up.

6. Prepare third cardstock sheet

Repeat steps 2–4 with the 10½" (27cm) sheet of cardstock (but score at 3½" [9cm] instead of 3¾" [9.5cm]). Add adhesive to the center square on your second sheet of cardstock (the one with pockets). Attach the center square of the third sheet to the second sheet of cardstock. Make sure the pockets are facing up. You should now have the three sheets of cardstock stacked, two with pockets.

7. Create patterned paper lid

Score the sheet of patterned paper 1⅞" (5cm) from the left. Turn the sheet 90 degrees and repeat. Then repeat on the other two sides. Next, on the bottom right corner square, cut along the score line on the square's left side. Repeat on the other three corners, turning the paper 90 degrees each time. Fold the paper at all the score lines so the sides of the lid stick up. (If your paper is single-sided make sure the pattern faces down). Then, starting back at your first corner square, tuck it behind the side of the lid and attach. Repeat with the other three corners.

8. Embellish and fold up box

Make tags to fit inside the pockets and add photos and embellishments to them. Also embellish your box as desired. To fold up the box, take the two bottom corner squares and bend the diagonal score lines into mountain folds (sticking up). Fold the two corners in and overlap them. Attach a paper clip to hold the corners while you do the other side, if needed. Repeat these steps on the opposite side of the box. Add your lid to hold the box closed.

Put a Lid on It

Don't forget about the lid! Add embellishments and alphas to decorate the top of your box. For my holiday-themed box, I flocked the words and snowflakes to add an extra wintery touch. I also added some thin red-and-green ribbon to trim the edges of the lid.

Gifting Your Box

Use the exploding box for whatever purpose you want! I loving giving mine at Christmas, but birthdays and baby showers also make appropriate occasions for gifting boxes. What about Fourth of July favors? Perfect for a little explosive fun. Also, you can use the box to house a little gift and just add ribbon on top. Or you can make the box itself the gift and embellish the center with a miniature tree. To create a tree like mine, cut two identical tree shapes (about 3" [8cm] tall) out of green cardstock. Trim ⅛" (3mm) off the bottom of one. Cut a slit up the middle of the other tree abd stop at ⅛" (3mm) from the top. Place the slit tree over the shorter one, creating a cross. Glue the tree to the base of the exploding box and embellish with bling.

Templates

When a project calls for a template, make a copy of the appropriate template below and cut it out. You will need to enlarge each template by 200% (unless otherwise noted) to bring to full size.

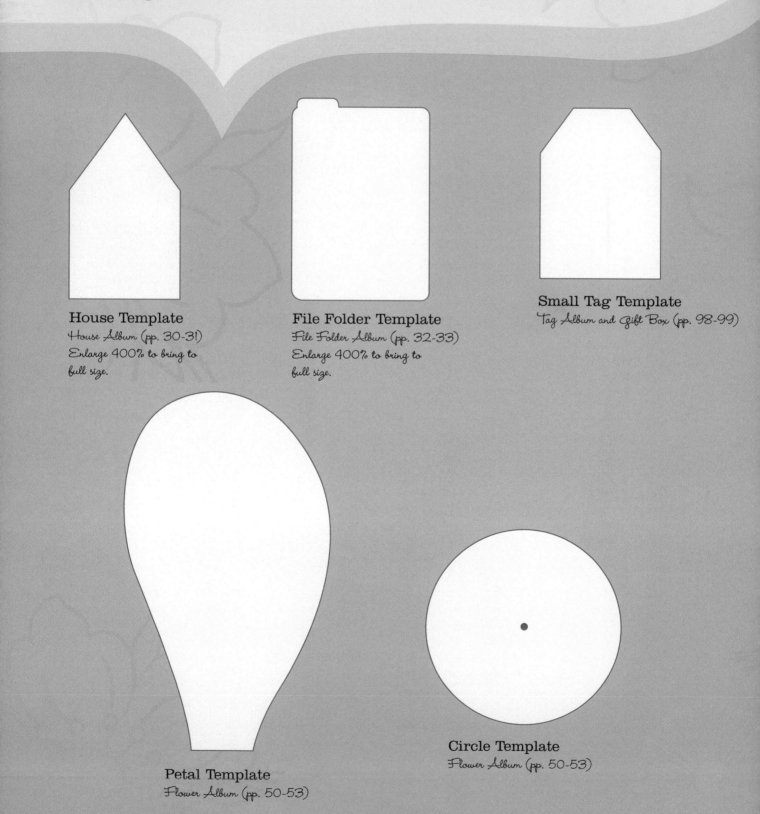

House Template
House Album (pp. 30-31)
Enlarge 400% to bring to full size.

File Folder Template
File Folder Album (pp. 32-33)
Enlarge 400% to bring to full size.

Small Tag Template
Tag Album and Gift Box (pp. 98-99)

Petal Template
Flower Album (pp. 50-53)

Circle Template
Flower Album (pp. 50-53)

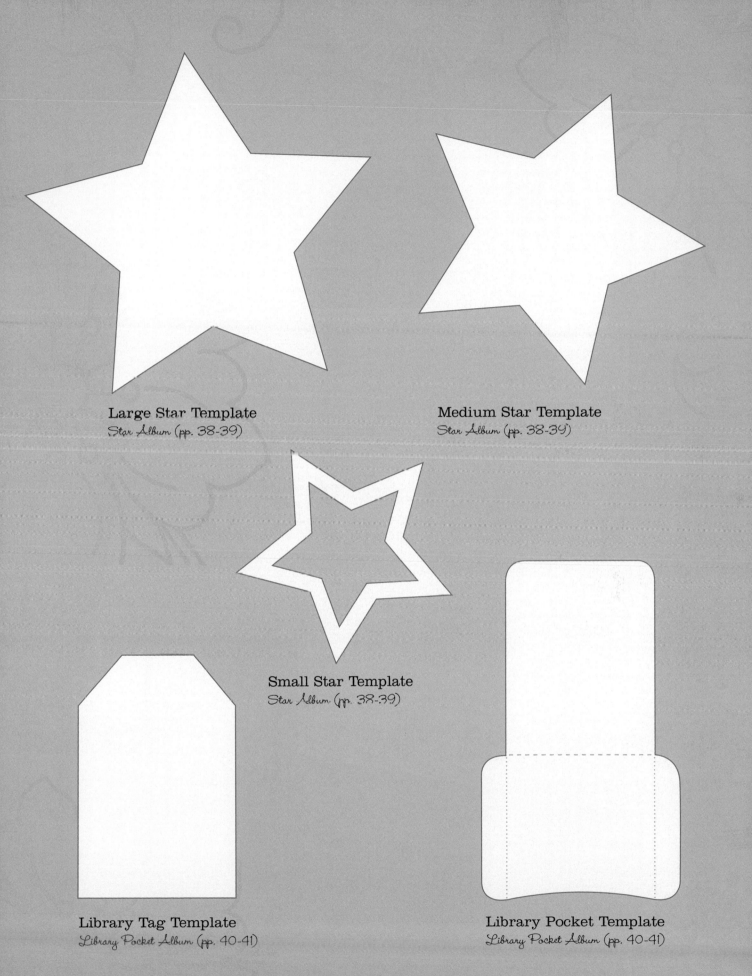

Large Star Template
Star Album (pp. 38-39)

Medium Star Template
Star Album (pp. 38-39)

Small Star Template
Star Album (pp. 38-39)

Library Tag Template
Library Pocket Album (pp. 40-41)

Library Pocket Template
Library Pocket Album (pp. 40-41)

Source Guide

The following companies manufacture products featured in this book. Please check your local retailers or go to a company's Web site for the latest product information. We have made every attempt to properly credit the items mentioned in this book. We apologize to any company that we have listed incorrectly, and we would appreciate hearing from you. Companies with an asterisk (*) after their name generously donated product toward the creation of the artwork in this book.

7gypsies
www.sevengypsies.com

A2Z Essentials
www.geta2z.com

Adornit/Carolee's Creations
www.adornit.com

All My Memories
www.allmymemories.com

American Crafts*
www.americancrafts.com

American Traditional Designs/Momenta
www.americantraditional.com

Arctic Frog*
www.arcticfrog.com

Around The Block
www.aroundtheblockproducts.com

Autumn Leaves
www.autumnleaves.com

BAM POP LLC*
www.bampop.com

BasicGrey*
www.basicgrey.com

Bazzill Basics Paper
www.bazzillbasics.com

Beacon Adhesives, Inc.*
www.beaconcreates.com

Berwick Offray, LLC
www.offray.com

BIC World
www.bicworld.com

Bind-it-All - Zutter Innovative Products
www.binditall.com

BoBunny Press
www.bobunny.com

ChartPak
www.chartpak.com

Clearsnap, Inc.*
www.clearsnap.com

Close To My Heart*
www.closetomyheart.com

Collage Press
www.collagepress.com

Colorbök, Inc.
www.colorbok.com

Cosmo Cricket
www.cosmocricket.com

Creative Imaginations
www.cigift.com

Creative Impressions*
www.creativeimpressions.com

Daisy D's Paper Company*
www.daisydspaper.com

DecoArt Inc.
www.decoart.com

Dèjá Views/C-Thru Ruler
www.dejaviews.com

Delta Creative, Inc.
www.deltacreative.com

Die Cuts With A View
www.diecutswithaview.com

Doodlebug Design Inc.*
www.doodlebug.ws

Dude Designs*
www.dudedesignsonline.com

Dymo
www.dymo.com

EK Success, Ltd.
www.eksuccess.com

Elmer's Products, Inc.
www.elmers.com

Fancy Pants Designs, LLC
www.fancypantsdesigns.com

Fiber Scraps*
www.fiberscraps.com

Flair Designs
www.flairdesignsinc.com

Gel-a-Tins*
www.gelatinstamps.com

Glue Dots International
www.gluedots.com

Hahnemühle FineArt
www.hahnemühle.com

Hambly Screenprints*
www.hamblyscreenprints.com

Hampton Art Stamps, Inc.
www.hamptonart.com

Heidi Grace Designs, Inc.*
www.heidigrace.com

Heidi Swapp/Advantus Corporation
www.heidiswapp.com

Hero Arts Rubber Stamps, Inc.
www.heroarts.com

Hobby Lobby Stores, Inc.
www.hobbylobby.com

Hot Off The Press, Inc.*
www.b2b.hotp.com

Imagination Project, Inc.
www.imaginationproject.com

Imaginisce
www.imaginisce.com

Inque Boutique Inc.*
www.inqueboutique.com

Jo-Ann Stores
www.joann.com

Junkitz*
www.junkitz.com

K&Company
www.kandcompany.com

Karen Foster Design
www.karenfosterdesign.com

KI Memories
www.kimemories.com

Lasting Impressions for Paper, Inc.
www.lastingimpressions.com

Li'l Davis Designs
www.lildavisdesigns.com

Luxe Designs
www.luxedesigns.com

Magic Mesh*
www.magicmesh.com

Magistical Memories
www.magisticalmemories.com

Making Memories
www.makingmemories.com

Marvy Uchida/ Uchida of America, Corp.
www.uchida.com

May Arts*
www.mayarts.com

Maya Road, LLC
www.mayaroad.com

Me & My Big Ideas*
www.meandmybigideas.com

Moxxie
www.gotmoxxie.com

My Little Shoebox, LLC*
www.mylittleshoebox.com

My Mind's Eye, Inc.
www.mymindseye.com

My Sentiments Exactly*
www.sentiments.com

Offray- see Berwick Offray, LLC

Pageframe Designs
www.scrapbookframe.com

Paper Studio
www.paperstudio.com

Pebbles Inc.
www.pebblesinc.com

Pébéo
www.pebeo.com/us

Plaid Enterprises, Inc.
www.plaidonline.com

Prima Marketing, Inc.*
www.primamarketinginc.com

Provo Craft
www.provocraft.com

Purple Onion Designs*
www.purpleoniondesigns.com

Queen & Co.
www.queenandcompany.com

Ranger Industries, Inc.*
www.rangerink.com

Reeves - see Winsor & Newton

Reminisce Papers
www.shopreminisce.com

Rhonna Designs
www.rhonnadesigns.com

Robin's Nest Press, The
robins@sbnet.com

Rusty Pickle
www.rustypickle.com

Sakura of America*
www.sakuraofamerica.com

Sanford Corporation
www.sanfordcorp.com

Sassafras Lass*
www.sassafraslass.com

Scenic Route Paper Co.*
www.scenicroutepaper.com

Scrappin' Sports & More
www.scrappinsports.com

SEI, Inc.*
www.shopsei.com

Sizzix
www.sizzix.com

Stampendous!
www.stampendous.com

Stemma/Masterpiece Studios
www.masterpiecestudios.com

Strano Designs
www.stranodesigns.com

Sweetwater
(800) 359-3094
www.sweetwaterscrapbook.com

Tada Creative Studios*
(888) 249-4304
www.tadacreativestudios.com

Therm O Web, Inc.
www.thermoweb.com

Tilano Decorative Products, Inc.*
www.tilanofresco.com

Tsukineko, Inc.*
www.tsukineko.com

Uni-ball/Sanford
www.uniball-na.com

We Scrap
www.wescrap.com

Winsor & Newton
www.winsornewton.com

WorldWin Papers*
www.worldwinpapers.com

Xyron
www.xyron.com

Zebra Pen Corp.
www.zebrapen.com

Zsiage, LLC*
www.zsiage.com

Index

> For more outstanding project ideas, check out these other books from Memory Makers.

See what's coming up from Memory Makers Books by checking out our blogs:
www.mycraftivity.com/scrapbooking_papercrafts/blog/
www.memorymakersmagazine.com/blog

Flip, Spin & Play

Step-by-step instructions on a variety of techniques show you how to create engaging, interactive pages that beg to be touched.

ISBN-10: 1-59963-018-4
ISBN-13: 978-1-59963-018-2
paperback
128 pages
Z1679

Outstanding Albums

Discover 50 amazing ideas for customizing pre-made albums as well as unique formats for creating handmade albums from scratch.

ISBN-13: 978-1-892127-90-7
ISBN-10: 1-892127-90-3
paperback
112 pages
Z0276

Show It Off!

With tons of out-of-album project ideas—like shadow boxes, mini albums and photo cubes—plus step-by-step instructions for different techniques, **Show It Off!** gives you the tools for putting your creativity on display.

ISBN-13: 978-1-59963-025-0
ISBN-10: 1-59963-025-7
paperback
128 pages
Z1937

Travel Scrapbooks

Discover creative ways to organize vacation photos into mini albums featuring your favorite travel destinations.

ISBN-13: 978-1-59963-008-3
ISBN-10: 1-59963-008-7
paperback
128 pages
Z0789

These books and other fine Memory Makers titles are available at your local scrapbook retailer, bookstore or from online suppliers, or visit our Web sites at www.memorymakersmagazine.com and www.mycraftivity.com.